Clay Modelling for Everyone

Pottery, Sculpture & Miniatures without a Wheel

Front cover

Bowls and lion. *The bowls were made by building up coils of clay over a form, (see page 24). The lion was made from earthenware by rolling a cylinder of clay around a small jar, leaving the head solid, (see page 69).*

Back cover

The squirrel. *This appealing squirrel was made by Rosemary Wren and Peter Crotty using a strong hand-building clay. The thin, hollow walls were built up from flattened coils of clay, which were beaten, and shaped with the fingers to produce the form. It was then biscuit-fired and decorated with stoneware glazes which were applied with a fine Japanese brush before a final firing.*

The flower brick. *This attractive way of displaying flowers is simple and effective. Using a stoneware clay, the flower brick was built up using the slab-building technique and then salt-glazed. It was made by Sarah Walton.*

Basket. *This sturdy and attractive basket, made by Richard Launder, was slab built with a coil rim using grogged white stoneware clay. It was decorated with slip, then salt glazed in an oil fired kiln.*

Page 3

Tree. *The tree was created out of air-drying clay. The leaves were impressed in a slab of clay, (see page 54), cut out and attached to the hand-modelled trunk. When dry the tree was painted with poster paints and varnished.*

Page 5

Rose. *Air-drying clay was used to create the rose. Flattened balls of clay were cut into petal shapes and a modelling tool used to attach each overlapping petal to the next, so forming the flower. A hole was made through the rose, and the stem rolled out of clay, attached with slip. Rose leaves were impressed in clay slabs, cut out and attached to the stem. When dry, the flower was painted with poster paints and varnished.*

Clay Modelling for Everyone

Pottery, Sculpture & Miniatures without a Wheel

EDITED BY PETER D. JOHNSON

Search Press

in association with
ARTHUR SCHWARTZ & CO.

First published in Great Britain 1988
Search Press Limited,
Wellwood, North Farm Road,
Tunbridge Wells, Kent TN2 3DR

Reprinted 1991

First published in paperback 1991

This edition distributed in the United States of America
by Arthur Schwartz & Co, 420 East 82nd Street, New
York, NY 10028

This book has been rewritten and rearranged from
illustrations and material in the following titles of the
Brunnen–Reihe series, published in German by
Christophorus Verlag, Freiburg–im–Breisgau:
copyright © respectively 1968, 1969, 1981, 1981, 1982,
1982, 1982, 1983, 1984, 1985 Christophorus Verlag
GMBH

English version copyright © Search Press Ltd 1988

Ton in meiner Hand by Walter Mellmann (BR41)
Kleiner Töpferkurs by Gerhard Frank (BR55)
Kinder Formen Ton by Gerhard Frank (BR182)
Kleine Töpferei by Gerda Hauck (BR189)
Ton–Plattentechnik by Ria Ruth Schafheutle (BR198)
Miniaturen modellieren by Brunhild Rebein (BR204)
Schmuck aus Ton by Gerhard Frank (BR205)
Töpfern ohne Scheibe by Erhard Dill (BR213)
Einfache Keramik–Glasuren by Beate und Stephen
Gorman (BR226)
Blatter–keramik by Vera Smeets (BR233)

The publishers would like to thank The Craftsmen
Potters Shop, Marshall Street, London for supplying the
items used on the back cover. The publishers would also
like to thank Richard Launder, Sarah Walton, Rosemary
Wren and Peter Crotty for giving permission for their
items to be photographed.

ISBN 0 85532 564 X (hb)
ISBN 0 85532 631 X (pb)

Typeset by Phoenix Photosetting, Chatham
Printed in Times, Singapore

Contents

Introduction

Clay is one of this world's great natural resources. Plentiful and unique, it has been used by man for longer and for more purposes than any other material. Malleable in its raw state, it can be formed into countless shapes and, when fired, it becomes hard and durable.

Clay is all about us, for it is part of the earth's surface on which we tread. It was formed millions of years ago from the decomposition of granite-like rocks that make up a large part of the earth's crust. Millions of years of weathering by sun, rain and ice have broken down these decomposed rocks, which contained feldspar, into smaller and smaller particles that end up as clays. Some of these clays have remained where they were and are now found as primary clays. Others got carried away by water. In transit they picked up mineral and organic impurities and eventually became deposited on plains and in river beds. These impure clays, which we call secondary clays, are mostly those that we use for making pottery, for they are highly plastic and easily worked.

Clay is relatively cheap and a wonderful material to handle. One can make a host of useful and decorative items with it: from bricks to jewellery, from teapots to washbasins to drainpipes. Clay can be gritty and earthy, or soft and satiny – it invites the hands to mould and shape it. It can be found in many colours given by the impurities in it, and can itself be coloured with engobes and glazes.

Clay, water and fire are the three elements of clay modelling, and they are all abundant. You might even say that our world is a world for potters!

Demonstrated and explained in this book are some of the simple but very enjoyable ways in which you can make things of utility and beauty from clay. As all the work shown is done without a potter's wheel it can be made without expensive tools, and does not require great skill: principally patience and a certain dexterity. The first pots ever made were containers, and were constructed by hand and with few tools. Neolithic man made crude artifacts out of clay and burned them in bonfires to make them hard. During those beginnings, nearly 20,000 years ago, our ancestors made containers to use, and figures to serve their religious needs and with which to identify. Early pots show decoration by scratching – evidence of their creators' delight and respect for the wondrous

Animals. *The animals were first modelled from solid pieces of clay, then cut in half, each half piece being scooped out, then joined again with slip and smoothed over. If fired, they should have an air vent in the base.*

substance that was both useful to them and provided a creative outlet. Nowadays prepared clays and modelling compounds are available from potters' suppliers and craft shops. Alternatively, if we wish to return to abundant nature, we can seek out and excavate our own clays for ourselves – such are the resources of the material we shall explore in the following chapters.

The main tool – the paramount one in every case – is the hand. In practically no other craft is the relationship of hand to material so important. That is why countless thousands of craftsmen potters – amateur or professional – find clay modelling such a satisfying means of self-expression.

Clay Modelling for Everyone is organised so that shaping, making and modelling is explained at the beginning and in the main body of the book. References throughout these chapters are made to firing and glazing, which are also described at the beginning of the book. All the work demonstrated

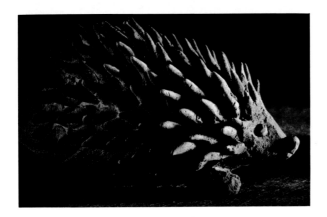

can be done at home, but if you do not have access to a kiln then it is advisable to join a local craft course or institute where such facilities are available. But the greatest joy of working with clay comes in the modelling and designing that precedes the stages of glazing and firing.

If you wish to substitute air-drying clays for natural clays, then no kiln is needed, for the majority of the works and ideas in this book can be made with them. Oven-fired clays can be used for some of the ideas shown in the model making section. However, and where applicable, the demonstrations in the book have been created on the assumption that you will be using natural clays for your work.

All the tools you will need for making the clay pots and models can be found in the home or made quite easily. A workplace can be improvised in the shed or garage, or in a utility room in the house. Working clay can be a messy business, especially when you need water to help the process, so take this aspect into consideration beforehand. Clay modelling is also time-extensive, for work in progress and finished pieces need time to dry out and places to do it without being disturbed: racks or shelves should be in places where your work is safe. These minor restrictions aside, you can make any of the beautiful and imaginative artifacts shown in this book.

If you have ever delighted in pushing your fingers into soft, infinitely tactile and malleable clay and wondered, what could I make with it? – this book will give you many of the answers.

PETER D. JOHNSON

Materials and tools

Fantail pigeon. *Red clay, or earthenware, is sometimes also called terracotta. It is much used for modelling figures, and when fired becomes a fine brick red. This fantail pigeon has been modelled in red clay and hollowed out, leaving some parts of the clay quite coarsely textured. The fired result is bold and striking. For details on how to make the pigeon, see page 93.*

Clays

Most clays can be bought from craft shops or directly from potters' suppliers, some of which operate mail order purchase schemes. For the beginner it is advisable, and simpler, to buy prepared clays from a reputable supplier. They are homogenous and stable, and each prepared clay will behave consistently.

However, as is mentioned in the introduction, natural clays occur widely, and for making practice models and small objects which you do not intend to fire, natural clays are almost as good. It is fun too, to prospect for these – geological maps will guide you to the suitable areas. Stream and river banks could reveal sources, and of course wherever there are brickwork quarries in the neighbourhood. Remember, clays provide a waterproof layer, the rain runs off them, sometimes wearing a bed away to deposit it elsewhere. Follow streams to stiller pools to find where the clay has collected. Investigate building sites, excavations and roadworks. Such clay deposits will contain impurities – sand, chemicals and perhaps organic material but nevertheless workable once processed to the correct consistency. Before taking away clay from such finds, however, always remember to ask permission.

Once you have your clay it is best to get rid of these impurities. Break your clay up into small pieces and remove stones, twigs or other foreign matter which you can see. Put the pieces into a bin or bucket and cover with water, which should be stirred from time to time over a period of a few days. This will turn the mixture into a thickish soup or slurry.

Using a garden sieve, strain the slurry into another bin or bucket in order to filter out the bits and pieces you did not find before. Repeat the process using finer sieves, thinning your slurry if necessary so that it passes through the smaller mesh. Let the filtered slurry stand until the clay sinks to the bottom of your receptacle and the water above is clear. Pour off as much water as possible and spread the clay to dry on a large slab (a plastic slab made from builders' plaster is best). Turn the clay over from time to time to assist the drying process. Store in an airtight bin or polythene bag when it reaches a workable, plastic state. If you intend to fire your worked pieces make a test tile and fire it to biscuit temperature (see Firing, page 20) measuring the raw clay tile beforehand to check shrinkage and possible warping.

Types of clay

As each clay has different properties from another clay, it is as well to know about them.

Primary clays are found where they were first formed by decomposition. They are sticky, finely particled and very pure. Being non-plastic (i.e. difficult to work), they are used for mixing with other clays as they are highly heat-resistant and white-burning.

Secondary clays include: red clays suitable for earthenware, which are low-firing; fireclays which are refractory (heat resisting); and ball clays which are used for stoneware and porcelain. To these clays are added sand, feldspar, quartz and other ingredients to make up the clays which form the three broad categories of pottery.

Earthenwares are usually red or brown, and are fired at temperatures between 700°C and 1150°C. When fired, the result is porous, and if a pot is to hold water it must be glazed or coated inside with some sort of water resistant. Earthenwares are very useful for modelling.

Stonewares are vitreous; that is, when fired the particles fuse together to give a non-porous object. They are fired to temperatures between 1200°C and 1300°C. Stoneware clays can be grogged; that is the addition of sand or finely crushed fired stoneware to the clay to make it more plastic. Knead the grog with the clay by spreading it on the workbench. Work your clay into it until the lump is consistent.

Porcelain is, when fired, extremely hard and non-porous. Made up of china clay, a primary clay and other minerals, it has the quality of being translucent when worked thinly. It is fired between 1250°C and 1400°C. Porcelain is not very plastic compared with earthenware or stoneware, and it is unsuitable for most of the modelling and types of objects described in this book.

Besides these clays, all of which need firing to make them robust and durable, there are other modelling substances, the advantages of which are that they do not need to be fired (although one or two can be fired). As they dry out they harden considerably, although they remain porous unless varnished and are not suitable as eating and drinking vessels. They are more expensive than ordinary clays but provide an excellent plastic raw material for those who want to work with clay but

Coil pots. The three coil pots in this picture are shown in different stages. The pot on the right, made with white clay, has been left to dry out. The pot in the middle is made with different coloured clays (rim, neck and body) and has been biscuit-fired. The pot on the left has been biscuit-fired, then glazed inside with a white glaze and outside with a dark glaze, and fired again. For details on how to build coil pots see page 34.

have no access to a kiln. These clays are called **air-drying clays** or **cold clays**. They dry out and harden quite slowly and so can be worked over a period of time. The drying and hardening time can be delayed by covering unfinished work with polythene bags or sheeting. Work made with these clays usually hardens in two or three days and becomes quite durable, when it can be burnished, decorated or glazed with a proprietory glaze or varnish.

Besides these air-drying clays there are other modelling substances which are less like clays and more like plasticine. They dry hard, some can be oven-fired, and they are best used for making little figures or miniatures (see page 75). They are expensive compared to the clays mentioned and usually sold by brand name.

As they dry out, all clays shrink and they will shrink further in the firing process.

All the figures and objects in this book can be made from the clays and modelling substances described above.

Preparing the clay

Apart from the air-drying clays and modelling substances, all clays must be prepared before you can make pottery objects from them. A clay *may* seem ready from the plastic bag or bin in which you keep it, but it is likely to have air bubbles in it and, equally important, is probably inconsistent in texture.

Clay that is lumpy and uneven is difficult to work, and trapped air bubbles will explode if the piece is to be fired. There is another good reason to put your fresh clay through the preparation described below: you get the 'feel' of the actual piece of clay you are going to use – in a way it is like getting to know a musical instrument before you start to play proper music.

Wedging is the term used to prepare large lumps of clay. It is a process of folding it over and over. Slap or bang your lump of clay into a block and cut it through with a wire or thick nylon thread into two halves. This is easier to do if you put your block on the edge of your work-table so that one half overlaps the edge. Take the free lump and turn it through 90° and bang it down with controlled force on top of the other piece. Repeat this several times, looking at each cut of the wire to see if there are any air bubbles or pockets remaining. When the clay is free from these it is properly wedged.

Kneading. Cut your block into shallow pieces which you can comfortably work with both hands.

Press firmly on the lump with the heels of your hands in a downward and forward movement. Pull the clay over and towards you from the front and again bear down on it firmly. This action again drives out the air and helps to align the clay particles so that your kneaded lump is plastic and easy to work. You can tell while kneading your clay if it is too wet or too hard. If it is too wet, kneading on a plaster board or bat will remove some of the moisture; if too hard, cut it up, sprinkle water on it and put it in a polythene bag for a few hours.

You will find that a rhythmic, rocking movement of your hands and body helps you to knead – the action is not dissimilar to making dough for bread, although the object is to dispel air, not trap it as in doughmaking. This action is sometimes known as 'bull's head' or 'ram's head' kneading, as the downward and forward movement of the hands produces the semblance of those animals' heads on the part of your clay lump nearest to you.

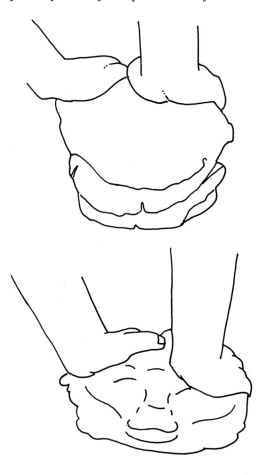

As air-drying clays and special modelling compounds do not need to be fired, no preparation of them is necessary.

Tools

Pottery is, above all, a manual craft and for making many simple pieces your hands are all you need. Pinching, shaping, patting: your palms and your fingers and thumbs can create a wonderful variety of pots and models.

For making many of the pieces in this book you will need some of the tools illustrated on this page. You can improvise by making use of household objects for shaping, moulding and cutting. You will also need a bowl or saucer in which to mix clay slurry or slip for joining clay pieces together. Slip is clay thinned with water to a creamy consistency.

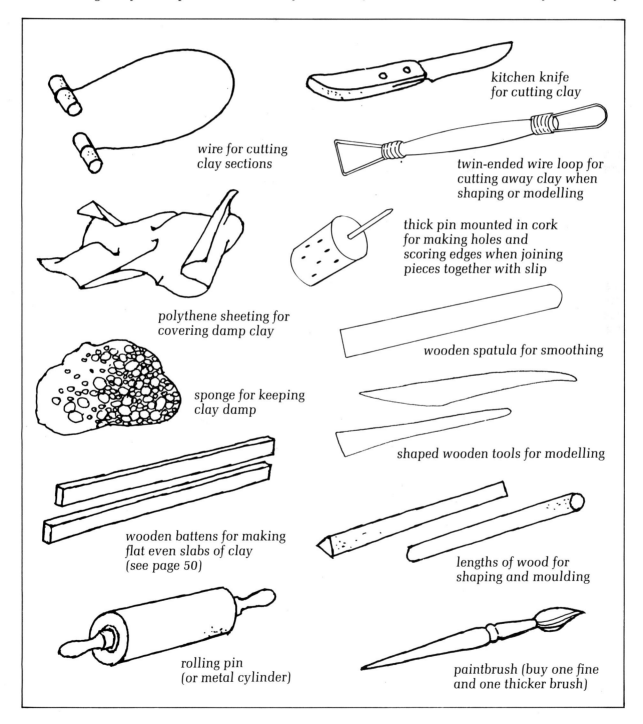

wire for cutting clay sections

kitchen knife for cutting clay

twin-ended wire loop for cutting away clay when shaping or modelling

polythene sheeting for covering damp clay

thick pin mounted in cork for making holes and scoring edges when joining pieces together with slip

wooden spatula for smoothing

sponge for keeping clay damp

shaped wooden tools for modelling

wooden battens for making flat even slabs of clay (see page 50)

lengths of wood for shaping and moulding

rolling pin (or metal cylinder)

paintbrush (buy one fine and one thicker brush)

Decorated containers. *These small pots have been decorated by impressing the ends of a wooden modelling tool into the clay.*

Also useful to have at hand for making marks are an assortment of household objects: buttons, keys, shells, nails, screws, old combs and forks, bottle tops – all these as well as plant material such as pine cones, skeleton leaves, and twigs. Make a habit of looking for objects with relief patterns, and keep them in a box together with your tools.

Workroom

The first thing to realise when starting to work clay: you are bound to make, at least, a bit of a mess! So if you intend to work at home, choose a room without carpets and soft furnishings in it. Many home potters work in outhouses, sheds or the garage: for those who do not possess these facilities, the kitchen is probably the best place, as there is running water handy when you need it, and the floor and work surfaces are easily wiped clean. Wooden surfaces are generally not good to work on, so if you have no other, cover a table with a large sheet of strong polythene. If you work standing up, ordinary table height is all right but if you work sitting down it is best to have a stool almost the height of the table top so that you can work on your clay downwards rather than at an angle. Many towns and even villages have extramural classes in institutes and schools where pottery classes are held. Join one if you can, for they are specially organised to cope with the problems of clay work.

Glazing and firing

Biscuit firing and glost or glaze firing. *The different stages of firing a pot can be seen in the illustration above. The rear pot (made of two different coloured clays) has been fired to biscuit. The pot in front has also been biscuit-fired, i.e., to a condition where it is hard enough to glaze, and then glazed with semi-opaque glaze.*

Glazing

The purposes of a glaze are twofold: to provide a non-porous and hygienic skin over the pot; and to decorate the pot still further. Glazes should be both useful and visually attractive.

In general, all glazes for all temperatures are made up of three essential ingredients: silica, alumina and flux.

Silica is the main ingredient of glass and occurs in nature as quartz or flint. Sand is crystalline quartz. It melts at 1,700°C and will then form a glass, but as this melting temperature is far too hot for potting, it must have its melting temperature reduced by the addition of a flux.

Fluxes reduce the melting temperature of silica; there are a large number of them with different properties, variants of temperature lowering and surface quality. Low temperature glazes naturally need more powerful fluxes than do those that melt at a high temperature. For our purposes we can say there are two types: stoneware fluxes for higher temperatures, and low temperature fluxes for use when making glazes which melt at 1,200°C, or below.

Alumina is found in several natural minerals and is the ingredient in a glaze which gives it adhesion and stability. Since clay itself contains a large proportion of alumina, it too can be added to a glaze to make it stiff and more matt.

Glazes

Those above are the three essential ingredients that make up all glazes. To obtain the various colours, surfaces and even textures, other ingredients are added to the recipe which itself is variable according to the specific temperature requirement of the glaze.

Glazes can be bought from suppliers in powder form. They are insoluble in water and must be mixed with it. If the glaze powder is lumpy, break it down with a rolling pin. Use one kilogram or 2.2 lbs of glaze powder with one litre, or 1¾ pints of water. Mix these in a small bucket or container, then pour into another container, passing the mixture through a sieve several times until there are no lumps left. As soon as you are satisfied that the glaze mixture is smooth, put it into a container with a lid on it, to prevent dust getting in, and label it, not forgetting to add to the label whether it is for stoneware or earthenware.

When you are ready to glaze your pot, first test it for absorption. Low fired earthenware biscuit makes a pot more porous than higher fired ware, and this will affect how much glaze will adhere to the pot when you cover it with the glaze mixture. If the pot is very porous, damp it with a sponge or spray. *Avoid grease at all costs – even the natural oils in your hands can make a pot reject the glaze.*

The illustrations show three ways in which you can apply glaze to your pot. You can hold it upside down by the base and dip it into the glaze mixture; you can set it on battens over a bucket and pour the glaze mixture over it; or you can brush on the glaze with a large, soft brush – a glaze mop, although this method of glazing does not have a smooth finish as it shows the brush strokes. For small work you can use different coloured glazes with smaller brushes. Most of the different coloured pieces in this book have been coloured with oxides and engobes before glazing with a clear glaze.

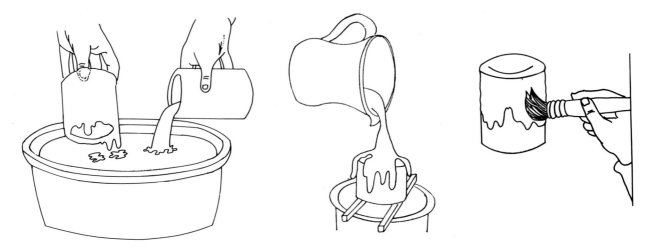

Equipment for mixing glazes. *You will need a scale, a jug marked with quantities, a sieve and a spoon. You will also need this equipment if you wish to make your own glazes instead of buying them.*

Testing your glazes. *The test pieces shown above were all made with base glazes and additives and tried out on different clays. Keep a recipe book and write down the composition of each glaze on the body, and the result when fired.*

Let your pieces stand on newspaper to dry out. Finally clean off down to the fired pot any glaze on or near the base by scraping it off with a modelling tool. Then wipe it clean with a damp sponge.

Glaze or glost firing. As noted before, glazes fire or melt at different temperatures; earthenware and stoneware. Never mix the two in one kiln. As the glazes must melt and adhere to the pot you must leave room around each when putting them into the kiln.

Stand earthenware pieces on kiln furniture (little trivets of high-fired ceramic) so that if the glaze runs it will not stick the pot to the kiln base or shelf.

Stoneware glazed pots cannot be fired on kiln furniture because the furniture will not fire to the high temperature. Make sure you clean off any glaze near the base of your pot, or the glaze will run and stick the pot to the kiln base or shelf.

Making your own glazes

It is outside the scope of this book to give a comprehensive list of recipes for glazes, but you can make your own simple, transparent ones from the four recipes given below. All the ingredients contain the three essentials for making a glaze: silica, a flux and alumina. A frit is a partial or complete glaze that has been melted, then reground in order to eliminate the toxic effects of lead or the solubility of borax, soda ash and other side effects that could be present if the raw chemicals were handled and mixed with water.

Transparent glazes
Recipe 1
Firing temp. 1,020°–1,050°C
40% lead bisilicate frit
50% borax frit
10% kaolin

Recipe 2
Firing temp. 1,020°–1,050°C
85% lead bisilicate frit
15% feldspar

Recipe 3
Firing temp. 1,100°C
70% alkaline frit
25% feldspar
5% bentonite

Recipe 4
Firing temp. 1,115°–1,145°C
70% lead bisilicate frit
20% feldspar
10% clay powder

As many of the chemicals used in making glazes are toxic, do not make glazes in the kitchen or where there is food. It is advisable also to wear a surgical mask to prevent inhalation of the dust.

Colouring glazes

A basic glaze for colouring can be made from 85% feldspar and 15% whiting (calcium carbonate). To this can be added oxides in small quantities and opacifiers – chemicals that make it opaque. The common opacifiers are tin oxide and zinc oxide. 10% added to the base glaze will make it opaque. To this mix add: cobalt oxide (very little, 0.1%) to give a blue; copper oxide to 7% to give a green; iron oxide from 5% to 25% to give a range of yellows and browns.

There is a wide range of ready mixed coloured glazes, available from pottery suppliers. These would save you the time and trouble of mixing your own colours. Don't forget to read the manufacturers' instructions before applying them to your clay.

Firing

Pottery is fired clay. We fire pottery to make it permanent, i.e. when clay has been fired it is chemically and physically changed and the change is irreversible. Pottery is not possible unless you have heat available to temperatures of 700°C–800°C.

To turn clay into pottery is a slow progression, for it involves the dispersion and loss of the 'free' water (which binds the particles of clay together) and the 'chemically bound' water (which is combined with clay at the molecular level).

A typical pot has three stages of manufacture. The shape of the pot is made and decorated by the potter. After this shaping and decorating, the pot must be dried out. During this process it loses its 'free' water and shrinks. Now bone dry, it is *biscuit*-fired to a temperature of 950°C for earthenware, 1200°C for stoneware. As the temperature of the firing is raised, the pottery loses its chemically bound water at about 600°C. As the temperature is raised still further the physical and chemical changes take place that make clay convert to pottery.

Kilns

Kilns are ovens for firing pottery and they are fuelled by anything that will burn to give the necessary heat. Simple kilns may consist of a fire-lined pit into which the raw pots are stacked. Potters in Africa and Papua New Guinea still make pots in this way.

Most studio or craft potters' kilns are today specially manufactured, and fuelled either by electricity or gas.

Small electric kilns, which will work off the home electricity supply, have a capacity of about one cubic foot. However, if there are potter's classes at your local institute it is best to join and so obtain the benefit of larger kilns and facilities.

Packing and firing for biscuit ware

Make sure that all the pots you are putting in the kiln are bone dry. Pots that appear dry but still retain some moisture feel cool to the touch. When packing the kiln it is quite safe to let the pots touch as they will shrink in the firing, but do not wedge them together. Leave gaps at the sides and at the top of the kiln.

Start building up the temperature slowly – 100°C per hour at the most. When you can see or measure a good red heat of about 700°C, then you can step up the firing rate until you reach the appropriate biscuit temperature (950°C for earthenware, 1200°C for stoneware).

The most useful tools for measuring temperature in kilns (apart from a pyrometer attached to the kiln) are Orten cones. These are slender pyramids made of special ceramic mixtures which are designed to melt at certain temperatures. They are usually used in groups of three and are set in a base and slighly tilted from the vertical. Set near the spy hole of the kiln a group of three may contain melts of 1,080°C, 1,100°C, 1,120°C. When the 1,100°C is reached the lower temperature cone will have melted and sagged, the higher will still be almost upright and the middle cone will have bent a little, indicating that the kiln temperature has reached 1,100°C, no more.

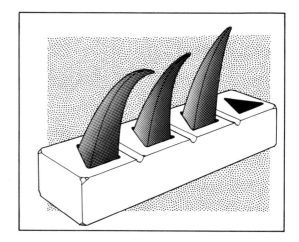

Biscuit-fired pots are now durable and hard. They can either be left in this state (undecorated models often look good at biscuit-firing) or they can be (and more often are) glazed.

Simple objects

Miniature candleholders. These candleholders for small or fancy candles are made by dropping balls of clay on to the working surface, and then pushing the candle into the ball. Make the hole larger than the candle, because clay shrinks as it dries. Ridges are made with rolls of clay added and smoothed on to the ball. Conical shapes are made by rolling the ball with the hand into the conical shape on the table. Pinch and work the clay with thumb and forefinger to make a ridge to catch dripping wax, or make a collar with a thin roll of clay. Decorate by impressing buttons, nail heads, pencil points, or sticks, moving the candleholder round to produce a continuous pattern. These candleholders were not fired but left to dry out.

Soon after we become acquainted with clay and its properties, most of us want to make something useful. Children who have potting facilities at school are eager to make things that they can use, either for themselves, or gifts for their parents – and what better reminders of their skills and patience than mugs and jugs that are set on the table every day?

The objects in this section are made with the simplest of tools and can be attempted by beginners, whether child or adult. Also, when decorated and fired, they will be sturdy, useful and decorative. Some containers need not necessarily be fired (such as the candleholders on the previous page) but for use as tableware they should be fired and glazed, using non-toxic engobes and glazes.

As with all clay work, an essential is space on and around which to work. A good sturdy table top at a height on which you can easily work (small children find it hard to work if they can only just see over the table: so let them work on the floor!) is vital, while a large sheet of polythene over the working surface is quite satisfactory.

Before starting, wedge up and knead thoroughly the clay you are going to use, in order to expel air bubbles and make it consistent and plastic to work with. For most of the examples in this section a grogged clay (clay with added sand or crushed fired clay) is used.

There are two simple ways of making the pots and containers in this chapter. You can either use the pinch potting method, as described below, or build up your pieces over forms. You can either find these forms in ready-made objects about the kitchen and house (saucers, plates, jam jars) or make them with plastic containers. As a lot of pressure is applied to the clay over the forms, fill them with plaster of paris and let it set. This gives a hard support that will not buckle.

Pinch potting

This is one of the most elemental and satisfying ways to make containers, especially simple flower vases, and in the hands of some professional potters it has reached a high craft or art of extraordinary delicacy and charm.

Take a ball of clay and push your thumb into it (*a*). Holding the ball in the fingers and supported by the palm of one hand, very gently pinch the clay between the thumb and fingers of the other hand, turning the clay ball after each pinch, to work the clay from the base of the ball upwards until it forms a thick cup (*b*). Repeat this process, always

working from the base, until the walls spread outwards and upwards from the supporting hand (*c*). Do not overwork or thin out the walls too much otherwise they will crack.

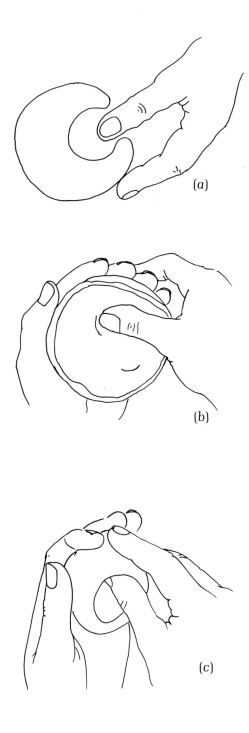

Decorated pots. *Balls of clay (right), impressions in a rope pattern (left), and little flat buttons impressed (middle), add style and decoration to three pots which have been shaped with the fingers. Note how engobe decoration on two of them makes them distinctive. The left-hand pot was biscuit fired only.*

Lion and elephant mugs. *These sturdy mugs, made by children, use simple straight-sided forms as a base. Clay was added to the damp clay to form the animal motifs, decorated with engobe and fired, then glazed with non-toxic glaze.*

Building around forms

Take your form and cover it with a clean piece of
thin polythene (clean food bags are good for this).
Invert it on the tabletop, as shown in the demonstration opposite, and put a slab of clay on it to
form a base. With a thick coil of clay form the sides
of your base. With another thick coil form the sides
of your container by winding it round the form,
smoothing the coil at the joins so that you build up
a sturdy wall. Continue to wind coils of clay
around the form till you reach what will be the top
of your container.

Turn it upright and place it on a stand. Holding it
steady, make imprints or decorations in the clay
with stamps, buttons, nail heads or any other
device which leaves a distinctive mark. Note how
the impressions are applied to the surface *away*
from your body – you can see what you are doing
much better this way.

Remove the form and the polythene lining
and smooth out the interior with wetted fingers.

Simple containers. *All the beakers above were made over forms (with the exception of the pinch pot, top row, second from the right). Stamped and decorated with coloured engobes, they were all fired and then glazed with a transparent non-toxic glaze.*

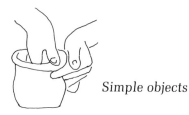

Formed pots. These were first made over forms and then shaped with the hands and fingers. The frilly rims were pinched out in the same way as making a pinch pot.

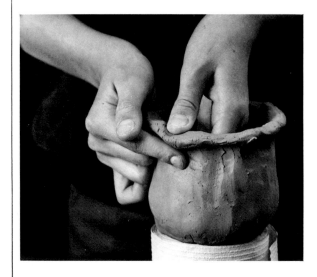

This photograph shows how to change the shape of a formed pot after removing the support. Using both hands, press and mould the pot with your fingers to swell the body and form a decorative rim.

Formed pots. *Pots made by forming them over saucers, pudding basins and bowls. The scalloped edge of the platter was cut with a knife.*

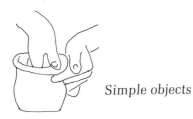

Jugs. *These jugs have simple spouts and handles. Decorated and glazed, they are sturdy and serviceable.*

Spouts and handles

Pull the spouts for jugs gently! Stretch the wall of the jug with wetted fingers; the fingers of one hand should support the spout while the forefinger of the other hand strokes the spout outwards

Handles are formed with a roll of round-section or flattened clay. They are usually easier to add to the container when it has hardened – otherwise add them to the pot while it is still on the form. Cross-hatch each part of the join (container and handle) and apply slip (liquid clay mixture) to each. Press together, supporting the inside of the container. Smooth out with a modelling tool or your fingers.

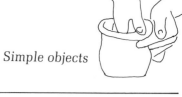

Mugs. The mugs illustrated above have fanciful handles based on parts of animals: a swan's neck and head, the tails of a fish, a cock and a cat. The animal bodies have been applied to the body of the mug by pressing thin layers of clay to the still-soft clay and working and smoothing with a modelling tool, then decorated. See how the black cat creeps around the mug to get at the unsuspecting mouse! Such application of decorative clay to the body of a pot is called sprigging.

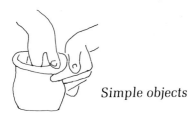

Animal candleholders. These figures are modelled over containers. They must also have air vents to the heads and tails, firstly to allow the clay to dry out completely before firing, and, secondly, to allow air to escape during firing.

When you glaze the figures, ensure that these vents do not get clogged with raw glaze, otherwise the models will burst in the kiln. Remember about shrinkage, so make the holes for the candles larger when you are modelling the raw clay. The elephant was decorated by scratching and stamping; all three models were painted with engobe or slip, fired and then glazed and fired again.

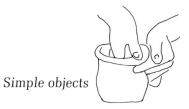
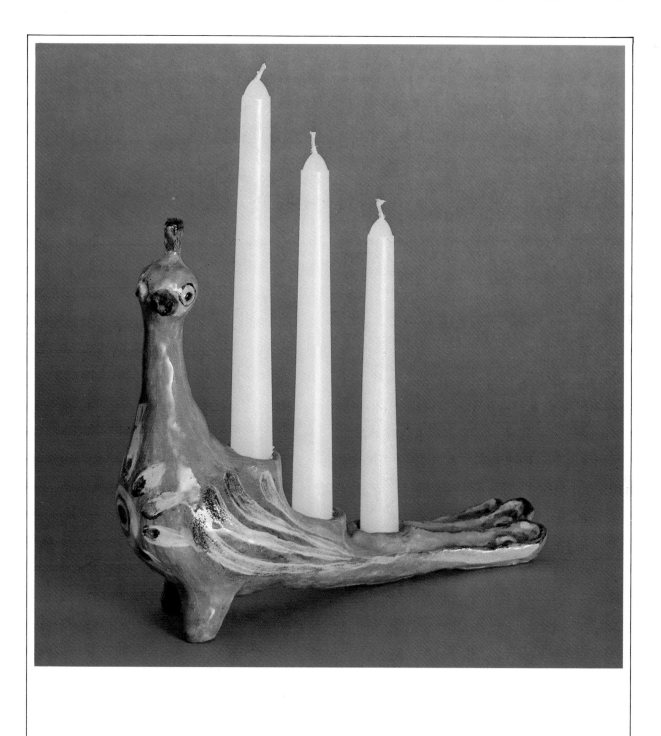

Peacock. *Two or three candles can be attractively displayed by making a larger model. Keep the shape simple and don't forget to make air vents to allow air to escape during firing.*

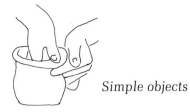

Egg cups. To start making the egg cups, use a couple of hard-boiled eggs to help you determine the size of the hollow they are to rest in. Then mould and shape with your fingers and a modelling tool the hens, ducks and figures you want to make, always remembering that, if you are going to fire the clay, it will shrink – first as it dries out, then again in the firing process. Allow at least 15%–20% shrinkage for glazed and fired pieces.

   These egg cups are robust in construction and decoration. They were decorated by scratching and painting with engobe or slip, then fired and glazed. Remember when making such pieces, that the bases must be broad and flat, otherwise when you come to crack your morning egg, the egg cup will topple over!

Building pots

Fruit dish. *This handsome platter is constructed by using a mixture of the various techniques described in this section. It incorporates the use of different coloured clays and has a most attractive alternating bead motif at its rim, which is made from balls of clay with a coil weaving in and out of them.*

The platter is quite robust, as you can see from the thickness of the coils: but care must be taken when bringing the rim outwards. If your coils are too thin, the outer edges may collapse on you. A simple glaze brings out the quality of the different clays, so that the finished dish has a rugged, peasant quality.

Types of clay

Pots can be built using balls of clay and coils. This exciting and robustly decorative way of making pots and dishes exploits the use of different clays. The chapter on 'Materials and tools' shows how there are different types of clay with different properties. Prepared clays from potters' suppliers come in different colours – that is, when they are fired. The important point to remember, when buying different coloured clays to use in one pot, is that they must have roughly the same firing temperatures. Suppliers' catalogues will always state the characteristics of their clays, so choose your clays not only for their colour but for compatibility. The pots shown in this section are made from four clays: dark brown, red, black and white, and are all grogged up to 25% with fine grog. When making pots of different coloured clays it is best to buy them from one supplier so that consistency and shrinkage during drying and firing are similar. This will prevent cracking and splitting.

Fruit dish and jug. *A dish made from coils and pressed beads of clay of different colours; and a jug whose body is built up from coils and finger-smoothed. A neck and handle from unsmoothed coils provides decorative contrast.*

Tools

A good working table top with a sheet of polythene stretched over it, a kitchen knife, a rolling pin or metal cylinder, a tape measure, two battens about ¼ in. (6 mm.) thick, plastic flowerpot saucers of different sizes and a turning table or box on which to rest the pot while you are working it – these are all the tools you require. A wad of old newspapers is also handy.

Making a simple dish

Roll out a lump of kneaded clay with both hands, moving your hands outwards and pressing gently with the fingers to form a roll about ¾ in. [1 cm.] thick. Coil the roll into a spiral, until it is roughly the size of the base you want. You may have to join two or more coils together if the base is large. Now put the two battens on either side of your coiled base and roll it out into a flat slab.

Take a flower pot saucer, place it upside down on the clay slab and cut round it with a kitchen knife. On to this circular slab place another coil of clay. Holding the inside of the coil, smooth the outer edges with gentle up-and-down strokes of the fingers. Repeat on the inside so that the join does not show. Be careful not to trap any air bubbles in the join. Now build up the sides of your dish using more coils in the method described.

Simple objects. These simple plates, bowls and egg cups were made using different coloured clays. Supporting the wall of each dish, fingerprint patterns were impressed into the sides. When dry they were then fired and glazed with a transparent glaze.

Kitchen utensil holders. *These cylinders show the variety you can achieve by alternating and combining various techniques with coils and balls of clay of different colours. The contrasts between smoothed coils, and beads and rings, is enhanced by the different coloured clays used. The jar·on the right has finger patterns impressed into the differently coloured coils of clay. The insides of these pots were smoothed as they were built up.*

Smoothed coiled pots

The pots illustrated opposite have all been constructed with coils. Their scale is shown by the rush matting on which they stand – they are quite small. The pot (*top row, left*) has been smoothed on the inside only; the others are smooth inside and outside.

The technique is similar to the construction of the pots shown earlier in the section. Make thin rolls of clay for the walls of your pot. Cut out a base from a slab of clay by using a flowerpot saucer or other round template. Then start to build up the walls of your pot as shown. See how the fingers of one hand support the inside wall while the thumb of the other hand strokes the soft clay downwards. Keep turning the pot in your hands as you work the clay smoothly downwards. For the inside of the pot steady the outside and work your fingers upward in a wiping motion. Keep your clay in a plastic condition, rolling each coil out individually from your kneaded lump so that it is fresh and easily worked. No slip is needed to join the coils to each other if the clay is properly prepared and is in a workable, plastic condition. When you have smoothed out the clay on each side of the pot, and made sure not to trap air bubbles in the process, you can repeat the smoothing process more gently.

The groove on the ashtray (opposite) was pulled and smoothed out of the tip by pressing inwards with the thumb and supporting the clay wall from the inside with the fingers.

Forms and shapes

When you have practised making simple pots and have gained confidence, try some more ambitious pieces. The diagrams indicate different forms:

1. Shows cylindrical forms, the easiest to construct.
2. Conical shapes, the walls continuing outward as they go upward.
3. The opposite of 2, the walls go inward.
4. Rounded forms of various concavity.
5. A combination of 2 and 4.

All these shapes are achieved by the way you place one coil upon another. Taper or shape your pot as you go along. Always draw a diagram of the pot you wish to make and have your drawing in front of you to remind you how to place each coil.

6–10. These shapes are varying combinations of 1–5. The beauty of coiling is that you can change the direction of the wall of your pot simply by adding a smaller or larger coil to the previous one you have laid down. When working large pots start the smoothing process as soon as you have laid down three or four coils, otherwise you will find the pot difficult to put your hand into.

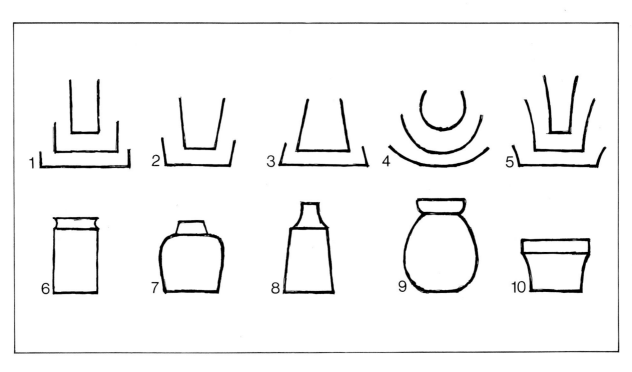

Coiled patterns

First roll out several coils of clay, then make a base and add the base coil, as in the photograph.

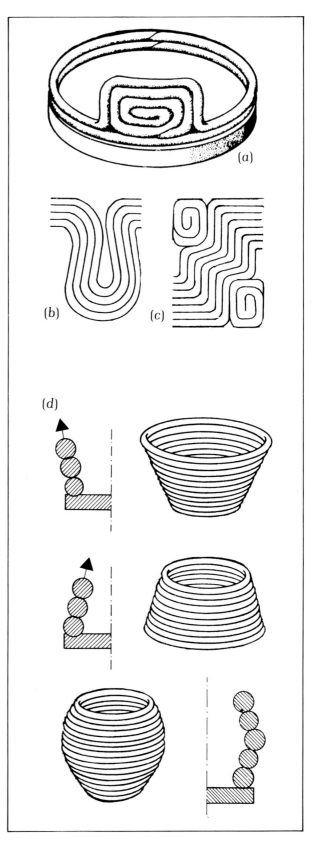

Then add a rectangular coil of clay to the base coil as in (a), and continue to add coils around it and the base coil. You can add spirals or loops at any time to your pot but remember that you need longer lengths of coil to complete a circle if you have such additions. The diagrams (b) and (c) show variations on themes. Remember always to smooth the inside of the walls of your coiled pot in stages as you build it up since it is difficult, if not impossible, to do so when the pot has grown to any appreciable height. Another variant is to cut out a section from a smoothed coil pot and insert a coil decoration into the cut, smoothing it in as before.

Coiled pot shapes

The diagram (d) shows how coiled pots other than cylinders can be made. Again, it is best to have a drawing or diagram of the pot you want to make beside you as you work. Your coils should always be of the same thickness: make several at a time for comparison and convenience. It is always difficult to judge thickness when making the next batch, so leave one or two coils on the bench to use as guides when rolling up again.

Patterns with coils. *You do not have to have the coils in your pot all laid horizontally, one on top of the other; or with straight sides. The three pots in the illustration above show different patterns and forms made by varying the shape (as in the pot on the left) and the pattern, as in the other two. All these pots have smoothed interiors; the pots at the back of the picture have been fired. The one lying down in the front has had its central section coated with engobe, then fired, then glazed with a clear glaze and fired again. These coiling techniques are explained on the opposite page.*

Fingerpressed coil pots

To make the fingerpressed pot on the right of the photograph opposite, start to build up the pot with concentric rings of coiled clay as shown. Place a coil on the base, and finger it down quite firmly, leaving a definite imprint in the smooth clay. Keep on adding coils of clay following the same technique until you have built the walls up to the height you want or until you wish to add decoration or new, different coloured clay, as shown, where the fingering technique is seen quite clearly. You can vary the decoration of your pot by mixing this technique with unfingered clay coils, or smooth areas, but in general a pot looks better if robust and rugged finishes are near the base and smoother ones nearer the rim. The insides of the pot can be left unsmoothed or smoothed. So long as it is watertight and there are no trapped airbubbles in your construction, you can vary the surfaces how you will.

Coiled pots made inside containers

An effective and simple way of making coil pots, and one that children enjoy, is to coil your pot inside a plastic cup, food container or, for larger pieces, inside a large plastic flower pot. The only condition is that the container you coil it in must have sides that slope outwards and have no restricting rim.

Make a clay base and fit it into the base of your container. Add two or three rings of coiled clay and smooth them gently, first to the base, then to each other. Do not press hard against the sides of the container from the inside, otherwise you will squash out the decorative pattern. Continue to add coiled clay in rings, battens, buttons and spirals until you reach the top of the container. Level off the rim with a complete ring of coiled clay. Leave until the clay becomes leather hard, then put a board over the top of the container and invert it. Your pot should slide out of the container quite easily, the clay having shrunk. If it does not do so, put it aside until the clay has shrunk and hardened still further.

Snail coiled pots. *To create the patterns of the pots shown, take coils and bend them into snail forms as shown. In order to make them uniform, cut several coils of clay to the same length (the coils must all be of the same thickness). Then add them to your pot to provide decorative bands, interspersing them with coils or smoothed sections as you wish. These two pots have smoothed interiors and have been made with contrasting clay colours.*

Making jug handles, and spouts

When you have built up the body of your pot to the height you want, you can add a handle by using a long coil, making sure that it is longer than you need. (You can measure it out by placing it flat on the table in the position it will take up, ensuring you have sufficient length). Apply the long coil to the top of your pot, crossing the long ends one over the other where they join. Press down gently over the crossed-over lengths of the coil and bring the two ends together. Bend these outwards and back to the base of your pot to form the handle. To make a firm attachment to the base, the handle and the base join should be scored slightly and slip applied to each surface. With your thumb, press the base of the handle firmly to the pot, supporting the inside part of the pot where the join is with the fingers. Pat out any unevenness of the rim with the palm of the hand.

When making a spout as well as a handle for a jug, you must position the spout opposite the handle. You can find the correct position for both by placing a rule or straight piece of wood across the diameter of the pot and marking the places in the soft clay. When you have formed the handle go to the mark and gently pull the spout forward from the pot with the side of the forefinger, supporting the outer edge as you do so. Finally, smooth down the rim coil on the inside.

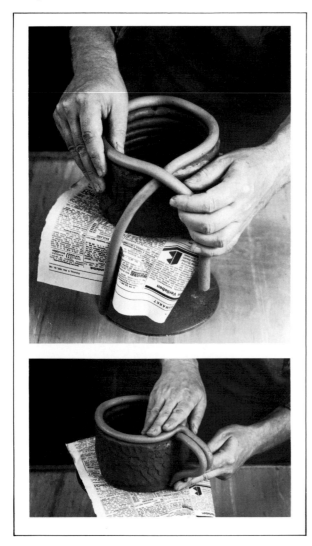

Jug and mugs. *These pots were made with contrasting clay colours. You can see quite clearly how the inside surface of each is smoothed down: the jug has an interesting change of texture where the coils have been built up to the spout. It is often interesting and effective as decoration to change the texture at a point where the wall shape of the pot itself changes direction.*

Pots made from balls of clay

To make pots from clay balls, first start with a stock of clay balls all the same size. The best way to obtain these is to roll out a long coil of clay to a diameter of ⅖ in. (1 cm.), then cut it into 3 in. (7 cm.) lengths, each of which will contain the same quantity of clay. Roll each segment in the palms of the hands, and thus you will have clay balls of the same size.

The three pots in the picture opposite were all made from clay balls, but they were used in different ways.

Once you have enough of the balls ready, start to build your pot by the coil method, using a base and a concentric ring of coiled clay. When you have added to your base the coil of clay, press your thumb into the balls of clay to make buttons, then add them to the first coil of clay. The clay should always be soft enough to work and adhere easily. No slip is used for joining – work each individual part of clay directly into the construction of your pot .

Now add the buttons of clay to each other, turning the pot round and round as you do so. Do not forget to smooth the inside of your pot as you continue to build up the walls.

Beginners may have difficulty in constructing these pots; in which case, build a coil pot at the same time to the shape you require. Then add the clay buttons to the pot from the outside, supporting the walls of the pot from the inside as you press on the buttons.

The pot lower left is built in such a way, but this time the buttons are pressed *out* to form irregular dimples. It does not matter if these are irregular but care must be taken not to smooth over the ridges created by the pressed balls. You can give each ball a final pressing when you have applied it to the pot, making sure to support the inside of the pot where you press it, otherwise it will become deformed.

The pot on the far right was made with half clay balls. Cut these in half and apply them regularly as you build up your pot. This kind of pot requires more skill as you cannot press the balls with your thumb or fingers on to the pot: the secret is to place the balls carefully next to each other and smooth with your fingertips from the inside to make the joins. If you find joining difficult, you can wet your smoothing fingers with slip, but keep your outside hand dry, otherwise your pot will get slippery and lose the decorative effect.

Clay ball pots. *These attractive pots rely on the effect of beads or buttons of clay forming the decoration of the pot. They require a certain skill and quite a bit of patience to construct, but are most effective when fired and glazed. How to make them is described opposite.*

Jug warmers. These are constructed so that there are deliberate air vents between the parts of the decoration to allow a free flow of air to the night lights which sit in them. Cut two bases the same size and make your decorative construction to sit without smoothing. When applying the tops, see that they have a large enough hole to put in the night light. The diagram demonstrates the technique.

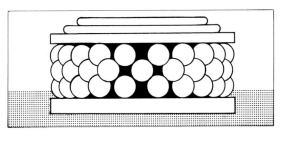

Plant tiles. *These attractive tiles are made from clay slabs about ⅖ in. (1 cm.) thick, and have raised and impressed flower motifs as decoration. They are made from air-drying clay, decorated with poster paints and varnished. To obtain impressed plant motifs, lay your plant material for impression directly on to the damp tile and roll in very lightly with a rolling pin. For the raised parts, roll out between newspaper a thin slab of clay ⅛ in. (3 mm.) thick. Into this thin slab press your plant material, remove it, then cut around the edge of the impression with a sharp knife. Attach it to your tile with slip. Press and role berries and buds by hand.*

Slab pottery is very satisfying to make and, in its simplest form, is akin to carpentry, for the pieces of clay you use to build rectangular pots resemble planks of wood. However, the fact that you can bend, cut and press into any shape, and twist slabs of clay provides an exciting medium to construct imaginative pottery of shapes that no carpenter or carver could conceive! Another bonus of slab pottery is that you do not need many tools – in fact the plantholder was made with two battens, a rolling pin and a kitchen knife.

The best sort of clay to use for slab pottery is grogged with sand or grog. If you are making large pieces the proportion of grog should be as high as 25 per cent, but less can be added for small pieces.

To make a slab of clay, place two ½ in. (12 mm.) battens on either side of your clay lump and roll out until your rolling pin rests on the battens, thus ensuring your slab has an even thickness. The

Plantholder. *This attractive plantholder was assembled from clay slabs rolled on a roughened surface to give texture to the sides. After cutting, the pieces were left for a few hours to harden. The surfaces to be joined were then scored with a stick, and slip applied to each edge before pressing the pieces together. When bone dry the plantholder was fired and glazed with a white glaze.*

walls of the plant holder have been rolled out to a thick slab – it is best when first attempting slab pottery to make your slab quite thick: too thin a slab will stretch and buckle when you assemble your piece. Cut away any bulges at the ends and you have the material ready for cutting up.

Most potters when making slab pottery will draw and cut templates out of card or paper to the shapes they want to assemble, so that they can place them on top of the clay slab to guide them when cutting out pieces.

Hanging plantholders on a rod

This variant on indoor plantholders is ingenious and fun to make. Make templates of paper for the plantholders from which you can cut out your pieces from the clay slab. Join the walls of the holders to the base by scoring and wetting them with slip.

Fashion a lug with a hole in it, large enough to allow a rod to slide through, for fixing firmly to the wall. Don't forget that clay shrinks in drying and firing, so make the holes for your rod larger when working the raw clay.

Make several bobbins of clay with holes in them for spacers between the plantholders.

When you have fired and glazed all the pieces, assemble them on a rod either by binding the rod as shown or with a combination of binding and the spacers.

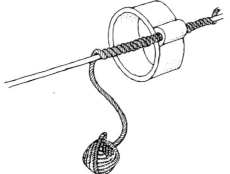

Hanging plantholder. *This is an attractive and effective way of displaying house plants. The plantholders are made from slabs of clay as shown, then fired and glazed before assembling them on a bound rod.*

TEA SET

This attractively decorated tea set is constructed out of slabs of clay. Make the slabs by rolling out the clay between two ½ in. (12 mm.) battens as shown on the previous page. This ensures that your slab has an even thickness. Cut away any bulges at the ends. No measurements or sizes are given, as most potters when making slab pottery will draw and cut templates of card and paper to the shapes and sizes they want to assemble. This is quite simple to do using existing pots as a guide, bearing in mind that clay shrinks during firing! These templates are placed on top of the clay slab and used as a cutting guide.

Teapot

Cut two squares out of your clay slab for the teapot walls, to the size you require. Then cut out the circular base, and the top leaving a hole just a little smaller than the intended circumference of the teapot lid. Work the walls, base and top into a cylindrical shape, smoothing the moist clay edges and joins with your fingers. This is the body of your teapot. While the clay walls are still damp, press leaves and stalks into the sides to decorate, supporting the inside walls with your hands.

Two smaller clay lengths are needed as rims for the top and bottom of the teapot. Cut out a circle of clay for the lid, remembering to make it larger than the hole in the top! Impress a leaf into the damp clay slab on both sides, then cut out the shape for the top of the teapot lid. Cut an oblong of clay and make the spout as shown in the diagram below. While the clay teapot body is still damp cut the oval shape of the bottom of the spout half into the

clay and using a skewer, pierce holes through into the teapot as shown in the diagram.

Leave the spout, lid and leaf shape and rims for a few hours to harden and then score the surfaces to be joined with a pin or a stick. Apply slip to each edge and press the pieces together.

Form the handle with a roll of flattened clay. Handles are easier to attach to a container when it has hardened. Cross hatch each part of the join (teapot and handle) and apply slip to each. Press together, supporting the inside of the container. Smooth out with a modelling tool or your fingers.

Cups

These little cups are simple to make and they don't have handles, although you can add handles if you want to, by following the instructions above.

Roll out the clay slab as before. Draw and cut templates of card or paper to the size you require. Cut two squares and a circular base out of the clay slab. While the clay is still damp work these three pieces into a cup shape, smoothing the edges and joins with your fingers or a modelling tool. Press leaves and stalks into the clay walls of the cup while the clay is still damp.

Plates and saucers

Using the same techniques, roll out the clay slab, and cut templates to required sizes. Cut out small and larger circles of clay. Also cut clay lengths for the rims of the the plates and saucers. While the clay is still moist attach the rims to the clay circles, smoothing the edges and joins. Press leaves and stalks into the damp clay to decorate.

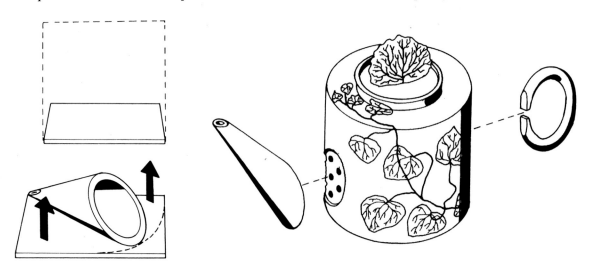

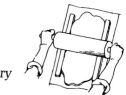

Tea set. *This attractive tea set with plant decoration is constructed out of slabs of clay. The pieces were decorated with engobe, fired and glazed with a transparent glaze.*

Leaf forms

Lovely platters and dishes in leaf form can be made by using large leaves from the garden and hedgerow. Rhubarb leaves are the best to start with; the shape is big and distinctive, and the thick ribs and veins are highly decorative

Using well-grogged clay, roll out a large slab on a sheet of plastic about ⅖ in. (1 cm.) thick. Now lay a large rhubarb leaf with the ribs downward on the slab and gently press it with your hands into the slab. Do not press too hard otherwise the clay will split. Cut the clay around the edges of the leaf and lift and stretch the edges gently upward to form the three-dimensional shape of the leaf. Do this around the edge until it is formed into a natural leaf shape. Use another leaf to guide you. Peel away the impressed leaf. Now gently raise the edges of the clay leaf upward, putting crumpled newspaper or plastic underneath to support the curved forms. This makes your leaf platter slightly concave. If the edges are too wide, pinch them together taking care not to obliterate the leaf pattern. Cover your platter with plastic which has holes in it to allow slow drying – quick drying will crack and split it. Examples of finished platters are shown on the next two pages.

Rhubarb platter. *This beautiful rhubarb leaf platter is made by the techniques described on the opposite page. In this case the clay slab was impressed with leaf patterns on both sides. Notice how the clay edges are quite thin – this is achieved in the pressing stage when the clay is pressed through the rhubarb leaves with the fingers.*

When dry, the platter was fired, then glazed by brushing on first a yellow glaze, then a matt green glaze was put over it on the lower half of the leaf. It was then glaze-fired. The finished effect is definitely autumnal.

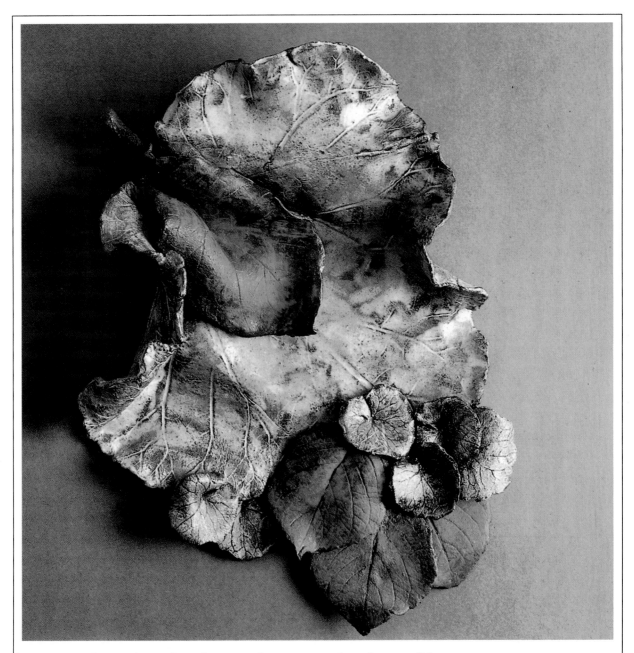

Composite leaf form. *This platter is decorative rather than useful. Made from black clay slabs of different thicknesses, a rhubarb leaf forms the main section or motif, smaller leaves being impressed out of the thinner slabs of clay, using the techniques described on the previous page. For the smaller leaves, lilac and small rounded garden leaves were used. Let each leaf dry out until it is almost leather hard, then attach the smaller leaves to the main leaf by scoring and painting with slip. If you want to hang it on a wall, make a hole in the top edge or fix a hanging lug to the back. Dab medium leaves with red and white engobe. Fire, then glaze the whole platter with a semi-transparent white shiny glaze, and fire again.*

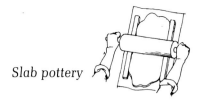

Mirror frame. This is assembled on a ring of clay from pressed leaf shapes as described earlier. Use a modelling tool to attach each leaf, which overlaps the next. Buttons of clay provide the fruit, which are attached with slip. Paint with coloured engobe, fire, and glaze. Fix a plain mirror to the back with strong adhesive.

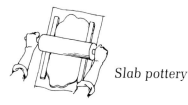
GINKGO POTS

The three pots illustrated opposite rely upon their decorative effect from pressed ginkgo leaves, also shown. All of them are constructed by the slab technique and, if you follow the instructions given below, they are easy to make.

Flowerpot

Roll out a large slab of clay and, using a circular template or flowerpot saucer, cut from it a circle for the base. Then cut a rectangle large enough to make the sides. Calculate the length of the rectangle as being the circumference of the base – use a piece of string or tape measure to check this measurement.

From a selection of leaves, find one that will distribute its pattern evenly along the edge of the rectangle, and press into the rectangular slab with the palm of your hand or a rolling pin. Peel away the leaf and there you have your pattern. With a sharp knife cut away the clay from the top edges of the leaves to leave a scalloped edge. Take this piece of clay and fix firmly to the circular base by scoring the edges to be joined and applying slip to each. Seal the rectangular join by scoring and coating it with slip and press together carefully so that you do not spoil the impressed pattern.

Dish

Roll out your slab and with two templates cut from it a circular base and the rim of your bowl. The inner circumference of the rim is the same as the circumference of the base, so one template can go over the other when you mark it out for cutting. Using the same technique as with the flowerpot, press leaves into the rim to form the pattern and cut around them. Now cut a narrow rectangle of clay the same length as the circumference of the base and fix it to the base with slip. Leave all pieces for a few hours until they are partially dried. Now fix the rim to the wall of the pot with slip. To get the slightly upturned edge of the rim place the whole pot upside down on a plate and press the rim down on to it gently. When the pot is leather hard, turn upright and wet the inside of the pot and press the stalks of the leaves accurately into the softened clay.

Vase

The two sides of this large vase are leaf-shaped, as an echo of the form of ginkgo leaves. To construct the base you need templates of paper and two cardboard toilet roll tubes. Squash the toilet roll tubes as shown in the diagram below. Using templates, cut out the parts of the base of the vase and assemble them as shown in the diagram. Now cut two large leaf shapes for the sides and impress each with leaves. Leave all parts until almost leather hard – the clay should be stiff enough to hold its shape, yet soft enough to be bent and shaped slightly without cracking. Score all the edges to be joined and coat with slip. Press together, leaving the outer and upper edges of the vase until last. Do not forget to leave an opening in the top of the vase. Finally, scratch the sides of the vase around the impressed leaf patches with a fork or sharp stick.

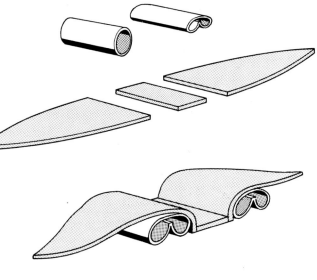

Ginkgo pots. *The vase, above left, the flowerpot, above right, and the dish show how you can construct a simple pot with leaf decoration. They were painted with engobe, fired, and glazed with a transparent glaze. Invent your own shapes and decorations by cutting out trial templates beforehand to understand the ways you will construct them.*

Table lamp

Slab construction is ideal for making any box-like construction, and this sturdy table lamp, shown on page 61, is no exception. However, because of its octagonal shape, it needs careful planning and, when being put together, will need to be specially supported.

To roll out the clay slabs you need two $\frac{2}{5}$ in. (1 cm.) battens and a rolling pin. For cutting out a sharp kitchen knife is used. A pin for scoring surfaces to be joined, a modelling tool for smoothing joins and a sponge for wiping the joins smooth are other essentials. Finally, you will want supports when assembling the lamp. For these you need a wooden board 16 in. (40 cm.) square with a large hole cut in it, slightly larger in circumference than your intended base ring, and a bucket or container for it to sit on. When you assemble the sides of the lamp on to the top and bottom, you need a sturdy box of the same height as the *interior* of the table lamp to sit on the interior of the base and support the top while you assemble the sides. This box or support should be narrow enough to remove when you have only two of the octagonal sides to assemble. (If you have no box of the correct height, build up a smaller box with thin wooden planks.) As with all larger slab work, your clay should be well grogged to provide stiffness and rigidity, both in the construction and in the firing. Very plastic clay tends to warp and bend in the firing. A bowl of slip is needed to fix the parts together.

The first thing to do is cut templates of paper or card to the dimensions you want. The diagram on this page shows no measurements, but you can make up your own so long as your supports are large enough. From your templates of the sides, cut eight rectangular slabs of clay, and impress plant material, such as grass, into one side with the palms of your hands or by gently rolling them in. Then pull away. Put these on one side, then cut out the top and bottom of the octagonal 'box' of the lamp from your template, and cut a hole in the top. Finally, cut the light bulb support to fit the hole, and a base ring which should be larger than the bulb support. Join these to form rings.

N.B. You may want to thread an electric flex through the lamp, in which case cut a hole in the lower octagon to one side before you start to construct your lamp.

All these pieces should now be put on one side until they are leather-hard.

Now bevel the upright edges of the grass-impressed slabs inward by placing the slab outside face downward and drawing the knife along each edge at a slight angle, very carefully.

Add the base ring to the octagonal base by scoring the surfaces with a pin, applying slip to each and pressing in carefully. Now take your wooden board with a hole in it and place it on the bucket. This gives you a stand on which to construct your lamp, for the hole in the wooden board accommodates the base of the lamp.

Add the lampholder ring to the upper octagonal part of the lamp by scoring and slipping.

Now put your box on top of the lamp base and place the top part of the octagon on it. By trial and error, build up the height of the box until it is exactly the same as the slab sides. Align the two octagonal parts so they match each other vertically.

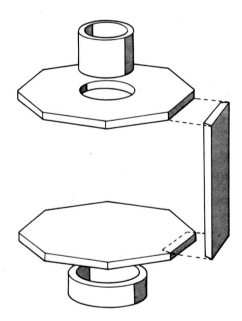

Take one of the vertical slabs and score and slip the top and bottom of the inside edge. Score and slip the edges of one segment of the top and bottom octagons and press the slab firmly in place. Now score and slip one vertical edge of this first slab, then repeat the process with the second slab, scoring and slipping all the edges which are to be joined. Make sure that the second slab fits and is joined securely to the first slab. Continue building up the sides of the lampholder until only two sides are left unfinished. Take out the box from inside the lamp as there are enough sides assembled to support the rest of the lamp's construction.

When you have finished constructing the lamp in this way check all the joins and wipe them clean and smooth with a wetted sponge. Leave until thoroughly dry, then fire and glaze as you wish.

Octagonal lamp. *This was constructed by the method described on the opposite page. The whole of the lamp was painted with a buff coloured engobe. The grass impressions were painted in with a dark brown engobe. When dry the lamp was biscuit fired, glazed with a transparent glaze and fired again.*

Three vases

The round vase is constructed of two circles of slab clay. The wall between them is a narrow rectangle which is joined to the circles about ⅖ in. (1 cm.) inside their circumference, a hole being left at the top. The supports at the base are two small rectangles of clay set into the rectangular wall and protruding beyond the circles to form sturdy feet. Scratch circles on to the main sides of the vase with a tool and fill with a coloured engobe. Leave it to dry, fire, and glaze.

The other two vases were constructed out of slabs in the manner described in the diagrams below. The front vase is cut out of an irregular slab of clay, rolled on a rolling pin and affixed to two circular bases, as shown in the two left-hand drawings. The other vase is made by the technique shown in the right-hand diagram, then opened out at the top end. Thick horizontal scratches decorate the outside.

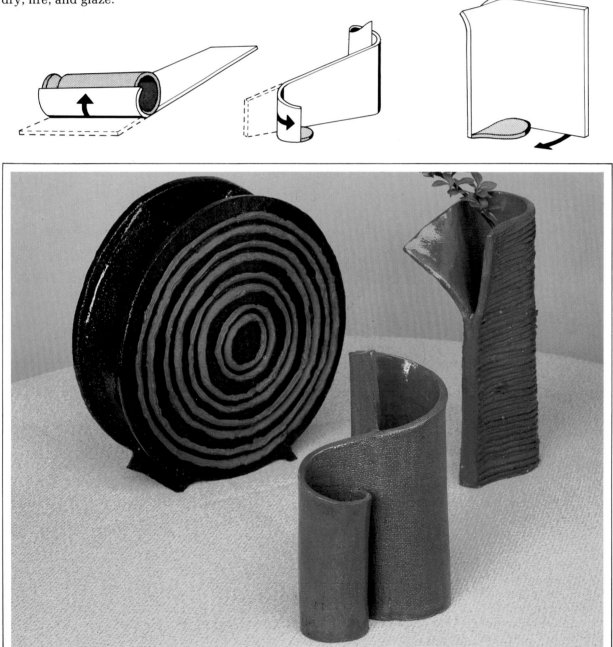

Simple models

Feeding time! *All the models shown in this chapter are simple and fun to make. Children and adults will enjoy creating these birds, animals and figures. All that is needed is a little imagination, some clay and a few tools.*

Basic techniques

There is no better way to familiarise yourself with clay than to make simple models of figures and animals as shown in this section. The best clay to use for these should be quite plastic or pliable – it helps if your clay has some sand or grog (finely ground biscuit-fired clay) in it. If you are using air-dried clay or modelling compound this should not be mixed with anything else. All the tools and equipment you need are your hands, a stick with a sharp point, and a tabletop covered with a sheet of polythene so that your clay does not dry out when you are working it. Useful too is a saucer in which to mix clay slurry or slip for joining the pieces of your model together.

Take some of your prepared clay   break from it a piece large enough to make an animal body. Roll it out on the covered table with your hand so that it forms a body. A carrot shape will provide a body for a lizard, crocodile or fish; a cylinder could be the beginnings of a four-legged animal or human body. A pear-shaped body can be formed in the hand by taking a ball of clay and squeezing it gently with your fingers until it becomes elongated and pointed.

When making larger figures it is important to make them hollow so they are not too heavy. Make sure you do not seal up the hollow forms, otherwise they will crack, or even explode in the kiln when they are fired.

To join two or more pieces of modelled clay together, first place one part against another to find out the correct position. Then with your stick score the two faces of the join in a crisscross fashion and apply slip to each face and push together carefully. If you do not score and slip-coat your joins you will find that the two pieces will come apart as your model dries out.

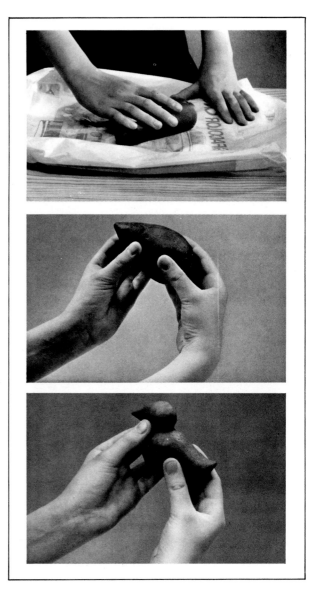

Simple models. *The pieces shown in the top photograph were made by schoolchildren. Although they appear to be crude there is a great sense of liveliness and expression in these little models. When you first work clay to make such models do not try too hard for refinement of detail or representational accuracy but simplify forms and expressions in much the same way as these lively models have been produced.*

Simple models painted and varnished. *In the photograph opposite, the clay has been allowed to dry out; then it has been coloured with opaque poster paints and, when dry again, varnished. Such models made with ordinary clay are fragile: those made with air-drying clays are hard and durable.*

Elephants. *These elephants have massive, heavy bodies and thick, column-like legs. When making the heads, draw out the trunk from the head by squeezing the clay gently in your hands, keeping it quite thick, and curl it against the head in one of the ways shown in the photograph. Curl the tails against the body and stick them on with slip. Pinch out the ears with pieces of clay and fix them with slip to the side and back of the head. The tusks of the larger elephant were slotted into holes in the lower cheek. When the model was dry they and the eyes were painted with white poster paint.*

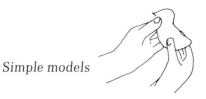

Feeding dogs. *What a lot of expression there is in this lively group of feeding dogs! Their shapes are quite simple, the differences between them being shown by the variation in the head angles, the tails and, in two models, the addition of lapping tongues. These models were painted and then varnished. The plate is pressed out of a ball of clay on the bench, the rim formed with the fingers.*

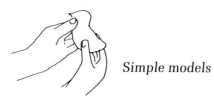

Armadillos. These armadillos are made from a pear-shaped body and head. The heads have been pulled out from the body and shaped with the fingers, the ears and legs being joined on to the main lump with slip. Incidentally, do not make animals' tails too thin, otherwise they will tend to break off.

Armadillos have well-defined ridges of armour plate over their bodies. Take a pointed stick and press it into the clay around the back and sides, then scratch each ridge with the point of the stick. Scratch patterns on the foreheads of the little animals and mark the ears. Form the eyes by pushing the blunt end of the stick into the head at each side. Finally, mark the claws.

Hedgehogs. This family of hedgehogs was made by different children. Each is created from a basic pear-shaped piece of clay, the spines being added afterwards. When making thin spines such as the ones shown in the illustration, use fresh damp clay, as they soon dry out if left exposed too long to the air. When attaching them to the body it is best to paint the whole body with slip before sticking them on. One child has chosen to indicate the spiny surface of her hedgehog by deeply pricking the body of her model with a stick.

Lion. This lion is larger than the other models. Make him from earthenware by rolling a cylinder of clay around a small jar, leaving the head solid. The walls of the body should be quite thick so that you can model the legs and tail without breaking into the cylinder of clay. The lion's features and his mane were carved and shaped with a knife blade. While still damp, the mane and tail were painted with coloured slip. When thoroughly dry, the lion was fired in a kiln to biscuit temperature.

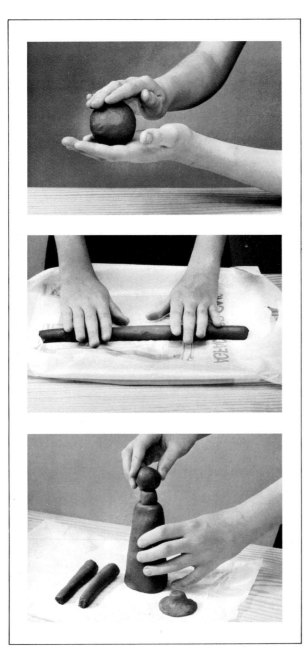

Making simple figures

The three demonstration photographs above show how simple human figures can be assembled out of worked pieces of clay.

Pat a piece of clay into a ball, then start rolling it on the polythene covered table to produce a roll of clay. When rolling clay this way, you may find that the pressure of your hands makes it uneven, or breaks the roll. The trick is to use only your fingers

Start with both hands in the middle of the roll and, with fingers slightly spread apart, roll the clay lightly backwards and forwards in a swimming motion, moving the fingers outwards along the roll to stretch and thin it. In this way you spread the clay evenly along the roll. Make sure your hands move in unison, otherwise you will break your roll.

From such rolls you can build up figures, as shown. Do not forget to score the surfaces at the joins and add slip to each face before joining the pieces together.

A visit to the zoo. *This jolly group of figures was made with terracotta, a kind of earthenware clay. They were produced for a school's project in which each child was asked to make one figure on the subject of 'a visit to the zoo'. When all the figures were finished they were grouped together and joined by a strip of clay at the back. They were allowed to dry out until bone-dry, then fired in a kiln to make them durable.*

Pastry cutter animals. *Another way of making models of animals is to utilise pastry cutters of animal shapes. They are harder to come by these days but can still be found in the specialist kitchenware shops. Roll out a thick slab of prepared clay, then cut out the shapes. Take the animal shape and mould it with your fingers to make it more rounded and three-dimensional. The animals above were coated and decorated with coloured slip or engobe and then fired to biscuit temperature. They were then glazed and re-fired.*

Chess set. *All these chess figures were modelled by using the techniques described previously. Remember to make the larger figures hollow and do not seal up the clay or they will crack, or even explode, when fired. The set illustrated above was decorated with white and black slip or engobe, fired, glazed and fired again.*

If you are using air-dried clays you can colour them with poster paints when they are dry, and then varnish them.

Painting and glazing

Paint your models in bright colours with poster paints or, if you are going to fire them, with coloured slip. When painting them put your figure on to a board or slab of clay so that you can turn your model around without having to touch it with your fingers.

If your model is made of air-drying clay or has been fired, you can varnish it with a brush or dip it into a clear glaze and fire it again. If you are glazing an already fired model, fill a jug or container with glaze, as shown here, and dip the model quickly – in and out once only otherwise the glaze will be too thick. Do not forget to wipe the base of your model (the feet, in the case of most models) otherwise it will fuse with the floor of the kiln.

Miniature models

Display. Individual miniature models are seen at their best in a special display cabinet. This one was made from an old printers' type tray. If your figures get dusty it is simpler to swish them carefully in a bowl of well-diluted washing-up solution and leave to dry – but only if they have been varnished in the first place.

Materials

Miniature models are fun to make. They do not need expensive equipment – in fact the models and figures in this section are not made with clay and fired. They are made with modelling compound, which is air-drying, so that they can be coloured afterwards with poster paints and then varnished. Miniature models are smaller than the animals and figures on pages 63–74, which makes them easier to work for small hands; likewise those who enjoy meticulous detail will find making miniatures rewarding.

It is best to start on simple figures. As in all clay and modelling work, the first thing to master is the feel and handling properties of your material. When you buy a packet of modelling material, take a small lump and play with it: pinch and squeeze it, roll bits out on a table or slab, leave various thicknesses to dry out, prodding and cutting into them from time to time to test whether they can be worked when harder. Some compounds dry out quicker than others and, unlike clays, they cannot be resoftened successfully. This means your work has to be direct and thought out beforehand.

Only take enough modelling compound out of the packet for your immediate needs (remember to seal up the packet immediately or the air will get to the bulk of it and dry it out). To keep the compound you are using plastic and flexible, wrap it in a damp cloth to prevent the air getting at it. Modelling compound is not cheap, and should always be stored in an airtight polythene bag when not being used. Apart from a non-porous table top on which to work, the tools you need are quite inexpensive and simple.

Tools and equipment

Illustrated below are the basic tools and equipment you will need to make the models and figures shown in this chapter. *Left*: packet of modelling compound; *top middle*: poster paints and palette; *below middle (from left to right)*: pot of varnish, craft or sharp kitchen knife, modelling tool in pen holder (this can be a strong pen nib or lino cutting tool), tweezers, tube of cellulose glue; *right*: fine and medium paint brushes.

Once opened, keep your modelling compound in another airtight polythene bag to stop the air getting to it. A damp rag to wrap your work in if you have to leave it, and a saucer of water to dip your fingertips in, are also useful.

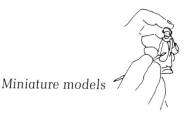

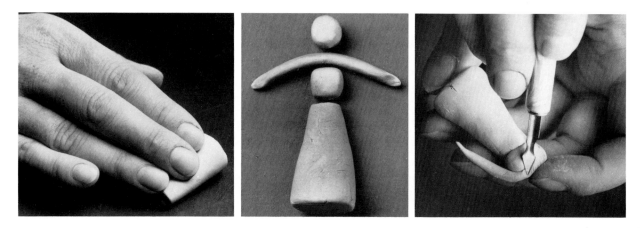

Making a figure

Roll out sufficient modelling compound as shown above to make the lower body. Make separate pieces for the head, arms and upper body, join them together immediately by pressing them together and smoothing the joins over with your modelling tool. If you find that your sections dry out too quickly, glue them together. Remember to set the arms in the position you want them to hold.

Clothing the figure

If you want to make the clothes of your miniature models more three-dimensional it is best to add pieces rather than try to mould them with your fingers. Take a ball of modelling compound and flatten it until it is quite thin. Then cut out the shape of the addition with a sharp knife or modelling tool (the two photographs below show how useful a pointed tool or linocutter is for this work). Such cut-out pieces are fragile, so leave them to harden before you attach them to your figure. In the illustrations a girl's bow is being cut out and fixed to the model with cellulose glue.

Sometimes such additions have to be moulded to the figure. Then you must cut them out and work them while the modelling compound is still soft and plastic. When working with modelling compound in this way you must plan beforehand what you want your model to look like – merely painted or more three-dimensional. If you are designing a group of figures they should be uniform in overall design – but not necessarily in expression, for it is the individual articulation of the models and their faces that give liveliness to a group.

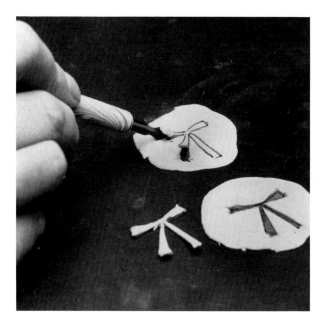

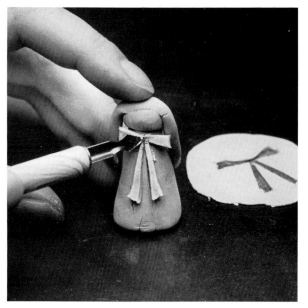

You will get a good idea of the scale of the models in this chapter from the photographs on this page. They show how to make caps or head-dresses for the two figures on the opposite page.

Pinch out a small ball of modelling compound with the thumb and fingers making a cup the size of the thumb with a ridge of compound that projects above. Then with the point of a pencil or edge of your modelling tool press the ridge back to simulate a frill. Next, roll a ball of compound the size of a large pea to form the head. Let this ball dry out a little before fitting it with the cap. Smear the inside of the cap with glue and push the head into it.

You will see from the illustrations that the modelling compound can be worked quite thinly. Such work needs steady hands and the individual pieces must be treated delicately, otherwise they will become deformed or even break.

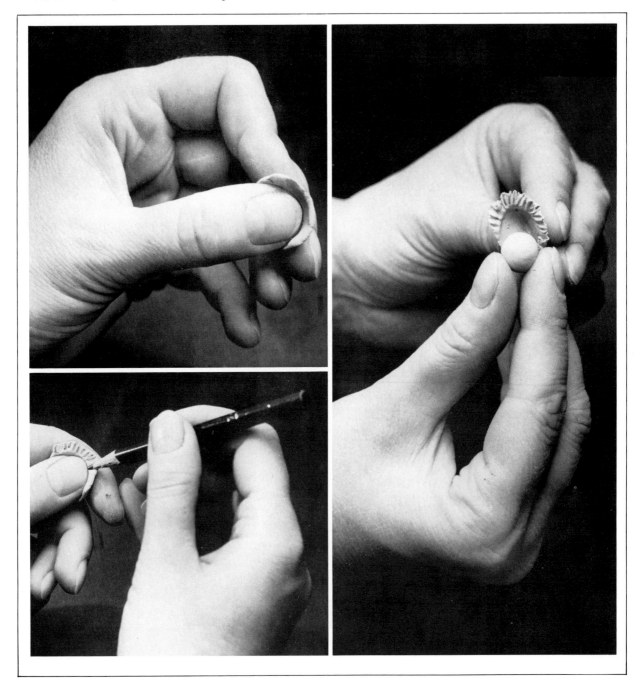

Little Women. *The various pieces shown above are all constructed from modelling compound. The size of the two women is 3 in. (7 cm.) high. They are very expressive and this is achieved by carefully articulating the figures in the construction stage. Notice that the features on the faces are not modelled but painted – two eyes and a mouth, that is all. Yet they are charming and quite convincing. The other pots and containers were made either by pinching out balls of clay or by the method shown on page 84. All these pots and figures were decorated with poster paints, and then varnished.*

Small romance! *The diagrams show how to make the little man above. You can model, rather than paint, the clothes. Wrap the body with a rectangular piece of clay, then add the collar and jacket revers. Either paint the rest of the figure or dress it and sculpt the hair. It is important to ensure that the arms of embracing figures should be flexible enough to bend naturally. For this reason it is usually best to leave them last of all.*

Painting and varnishing

Once figures are dry they can be painted with opaque water colours or poster paints. If the colour is laid on in strokes you can build up texture. When painting, hold your model very carefully, rotating it in your fingers while steadying both hands on the table. Start with the head and let each colour dry before applying the next coat. Some simple expressions are shown below. You can scratch paint away to give expression or texture before varnishing.

Use tweezers to hold your model when dipping it into the varnish. Let the drips run off into the container and stand the model on thick newspaper to dry. Varnishing enhances the colours and will also make your figures stronger.

Goosegirl miniatures. *This charming group of miniature models was made with air-drying clay, then coloured with poster paints and varnished. The photograph below shows you how to model the geese. The wings are added to the torso while the compound is still plastic – they are harder to attach when they are dry. By bending the necks into different angles, each goose is given its own character.*

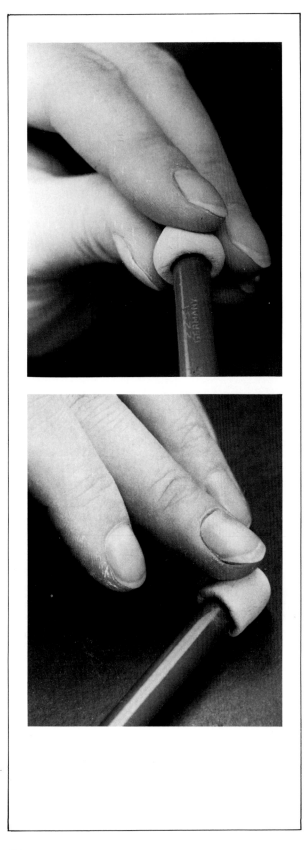

Making miniature pots

Take pencils, pens and other rounded objects from the kitchen. Make a ball of compound and press on to the end of the 'tool' you are using, then roll gently on the table as shown in these two photographs. In this way you can make the pots of different sizes shown on page 79 and in the colour picture opposite.

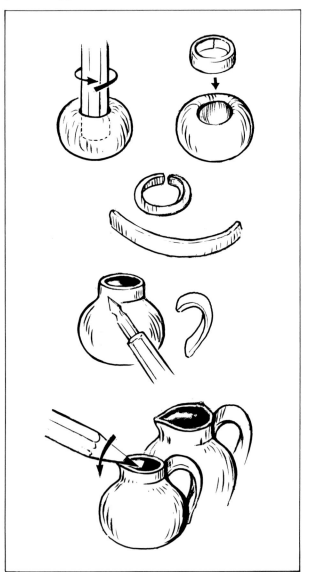

To make jugs and handled pots, follow the guidelines given in the diagrams above. If the compound instructions say you can use water as an adhesive, then wet each surface before pressing the handles and collars on to the body of your miniature pot. Otherwise wait until the compound is dry, then fix with cellulose glue.

Miniature pots and fruit. *All the pots here were made either by
pinching out from a ball of compound or by rolling around a pencil
end as shown opposite. When dry the pieces were coloured with
poster paints and varnished.*

*Try making the fruit by rolling and pinching lumps of compound in
your hands. Colour them delicately when dry, and varnish. The
grapes are little balls of compound stuck on to a core with glue.*

*When you decorate pots of this kind it is best to imitate folk or
peasant designs rather than follow delicate china patterns. Colouring
needs a steady hand and quite a lot of patience!*

Unvarnished models. *These charming miniature models were made by schoolchildren. The children used air-drying clay and the tiny forms were painted with poster paints when dry.*

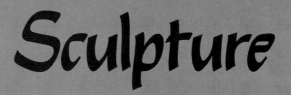

Mother and child. *Simplicity of form and shape make an effective model of mother and child. The forms were freely built up and worked out of clay, hollowed out during construction, then fired and glazed with a thin black glaze.*

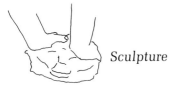
Materials

More advanced techniques are used to make the models shown in this chapter. All the models shown are to be fired in a kiln, so a word is necessary about the best clay to use for this type of work.

The clay which is most easily workable, and fires well after the model is made and dried out, is *fat* or plastic in consistency. Fat clay is not actually fatty but has a shiny appearance, is smooth and supple, tough, and easy to mould. One way of testing if clay is fat enough to model from is to roll out a coil of clay to about ½ in. (12 mm.) thickness and tie a simple thumb knot with a foot length of the coil. If the clay coil does not break or split then the clay is fat, or plastic. If it does break or split, then it is too lean.

To your fat, plastic clay add grog or sand. You can add up to 35 per cent body of sand or grog to good plastic clay without losing plasticity. Grog is finely ground fired clay, available in different grades, rough or fine: rough is recommended.

Tools

Your hands, of course. Plus a wire with toggles at each end for cutting, a double-ended wire loop for paring and scooping and a few modelling tools of different shapes (see page 13).

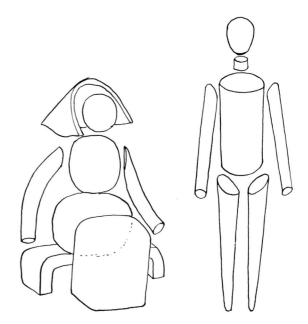

Human figures

When making human figures simplify the shapes as much as possible. Thin legs and features collapse easily. Work out the basic forms (head, trunk, arms and legs) on paper, and then make the simplest rolled forms as shown in the diagram above. Each large section should be hollowed out and air-vented. Standing figures are difficult and succeed best when they are clothed: seated figures are easier. the diagram (*left above*) shows the basic forms of a seated peasant woman, the skirt being the block form in front of her.

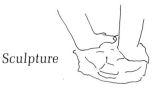

Girl with dove. *This charming model was made out of simple shapes. A thick roll of clay was slightly flattened and hollowed out to form the body. The neck, head, arms and dove were attached using hands and a modelling tool to shape and mould the clay. A scarf was draped over the head to balance the form. The model was fired, but left unglazed.*

Seated woman. *This simplified but very graceful model takes on the appearance of sculpture, of which modelling is a branch. This piece was constructed much in the same way as the diagram opposite. Each hollowed-out form, with air vents, was added to the others.*

The figure was fired, then glazed with a thin black glaze which allows the texture of the fired clay to show through in places.

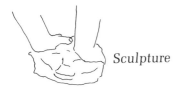

Baby. *A small child's body is differently proportioned to that of an adult – a newborn's head is in ratio to the body 1:4. An adult's ratio is 1:7 or even 1:8. When the head of the baby above was formed, it comprised two spheres cut and pressed together in the manner of the diagram on the right. The head form, as well as the body, were hollowed out before the features, arms and legs, were added.*

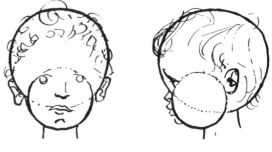

Boy's head. *Beginners to clay modelling should not attempt to model a head as it is not easy. Correct dimensions and features are only achieved with practice. However, this model has been included to illustrate what can be done with a little perseverance! Solid forms should be hollow and air-vented. As newspaper burns up during firing it can be used as a base to construct the neck and head as shown. Wrap clay around compacted newspaper, building up the form. It is helpful to use photographs and sketches of the model to achieve correct dimensions. Features are shaped using hands and a modelling tool and hair is sculpted on afterwards.*

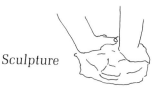

Animals and birds

When making models such as the donkey, the bull and the pigeon shown on these two pages, never attempt to make them look realistic. Thin legs and features collapse easily, so shape your forms chunkily and simplify shapes so that the whole model is sturdy yet recognisable for what it represents. Hollow out when you have got the proportions correct; shape further after you have joined the halves together; and do not forget to put in air vents!

After that, add features to your basic, hollowed-out body shape: ears, horns, wings. You can model the heads separately and put them on to the body later, first having hollowed them out, but, again, put in an air vent in an unobtrusive place. When making models such as these leave tool marks and slight imperfections in the modelling as they give character. If you smooth it all down, it weakens the general effect. You can see the grog in the clay quite well in the model of the donkey. Coarse grogged clay possesses a vital and interesting texture.

When modelling such pieces, raise them up on a large box so that you can turn them round without having to pick them up. The bellies of four-legged animals need to be supported with a lump of clay which can later be removed.

Cock. This proud bird was formed from one lump of clay. When its
body was made, it was cut with the wire diagonally above the base of
the tail through to the lower breast and the two pieces hollowed out.
They were joined and smoothed over with a modelling tool. The comb
and wattles were added and smoothed in with slip.

The tail is a thick slab of clay cut to shape and added to the body of
the cock and the base. The model was then worked over to achieve
the final shape; when this was finished satisfactorily grooves and
scratches were made with the wire tool and modelling tools, in order
to simulate the curved feature of the tail, the wings, legs, ruff and
comb. An air vent was driven diagonally up through the base and the
legs to the hollowed-out interior of the body.

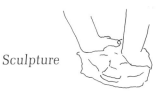

The Bremen musicians. *This animated and vociferous group was inspired by an old German folk tale. The group is 16 in. (40 cm.) high. Each animal was modelled separately and each is hollowed out – the weight of solid figures would collapse the pyramid!*

Notice how the centre of gravity runs vertically down from the cock's body to the front legs of the donkey.

When the group was made, each figure was allowed to dry out until leather-hard, and then fixed to the back of the supporting animal with slip.

Invent your own groups of animals that might tell a story. Before starting, draw the figures on a piece of paper to finalise the arrangement and, if they are stacked like the Bremen musicians, to determine the centre of gravity.

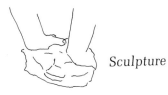

Pig. This chubby pig's shape is especially suitable for modelling as it is made from very few pieces of clay. Hollow out the rounded body. Make four stubby skittle-shaped clay legs and a skittle-shaped nose. Cut two three-cornered ears from a clay slab. Roll out a little curly tail. Attach these pieces to the body with slip, working over and smoothing all the joins. Don't forget to emphasise the round, cuddly shape of the pig to give it character and charm!

Clay ball necklaces. *These are easy to make. Roll each clay ball to the correct size, prick through with a toothpick or skewer while it is still plastic, making the holes larger than the thread, as clay shrinks when drying. When still damp, colour; then fire and glaze. Thread and knot on to thin leather thongs.*

Individual beads, brooches and pendants are small and require deft handling when being made, yet the assembled results are attractive and effective. Design clay jewellery to suit your own wardrobe, or make it for friends and relatives, having in mind their personalities and tastes. Young children can easily make their own jewellery and will wear it with pride!

You can make jewellery with air-drying clay which is coloured with poster paints and varnished, or a smooth plastic clay without additives which is fired and glazed. Other modelling substances can be used. These are usually sold by brand name. Always read the manufacturer's instructions before starting.

Always remember that clay shrinks as it dries out, and will shrink still further when it is fired. When you make individual beads or pendants therefore, allow for 10%–15% overall shrinkage, which means that the holes will decrease in size also. The size of the hole depends on what thread you use, so always make the holes in the damp jewellery larger than the diameter of your thread or thong. If holes appear ragged after you have made them, scrape them with a knife when the clay has dried.

Make several collections of beads of different shapes, sizes and colours, then arrange them on a thong or thread to give variety to your necklaces. The photographs and diagrams in this chapter give ideas on how to create a colourful assortment of necklaces and pendants.

For details on how to make brooches and pendants decorated with plant motifs, see page 103.

Decorating clay jewellery

If you make jewellery out of clay that is to be fired, then there are some useful tips to be learned. Because each individual bead is so small, any handling has to be done with care. It is best to have a selection of wooden skewers slightly larger than the diameter of the beads' holes, and with pointed ends. Push a raw bead on to the end of the skewer, then you can hold it to paint on your decoration.

A thick flat piece of polystyrene foam will serve as a stand for the beads you have decorated: all you do is to stick the free end of the skewer into the slab of foam and let the beads dry out before taking them off the point.

To decorate beads or individual pendants, use engobe or coloured slip. Engobe is a thin slurry of clay base, with an added colouring medium. Engobe or slip is easily made: put a lump of clay on the table, then press your thumb into it to form a well. Fill the well with water, then twirl a brush

Large beads being decorated with engobe. Steady your hands on the table top.

Biscuit-fired beads being glazed by painting on the glaze with a brush.

The quickest method of dipping beads.

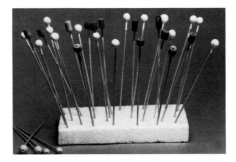

The beads on their skewers are drying out.

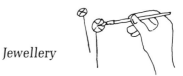

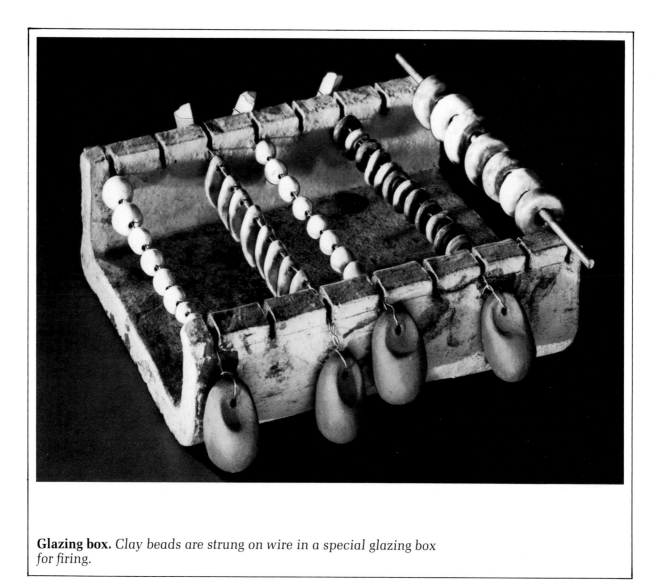

Glazing box. *Clay beads are strung on wire in a special glazing box for firing.*

around in the hollow until a paste forms. This is raw engobe or slip. To this add colouring oxide, which you can buy from potters' suppliers. A little colouring oxide goes a long way! – Be careful!

When making slip for painting jewellery beads and ornaments it is useful to keep a recipe book. Many potters will mix up several colouring slips in jars or left-over food cartons, labelling them with the mixture details and the effect which they give.

Colouring oxides are sold at most craft shops or potters' suppliers. As a little goes a long way, buy small quantities and keep them in airtight containers. Unlike paints, oxides in the raw state do not indicate by their natural colour what your fired result will be, but catalogues and lists available from suppliers usually give details of what colour they will fire to. Some oxides are toxic, so be careful with them: if you have any cuts or abrasions on your hands let these heal before handling and mixing the oxides. Children should be given prepared coloured slips and be warned not to put decorating brushes in their mouths!

Firing beads

Because beads are covered all over with slip, or glaze, you cannot fire them properly in the kiln on trays. The illustration above shows a special glazing box made from a slab of clay with grooves cut in it. This has already been fired. String your beads on chrome-nickel wire or on steel rods. Weigh down the wire at each end with a lump of fired clay.

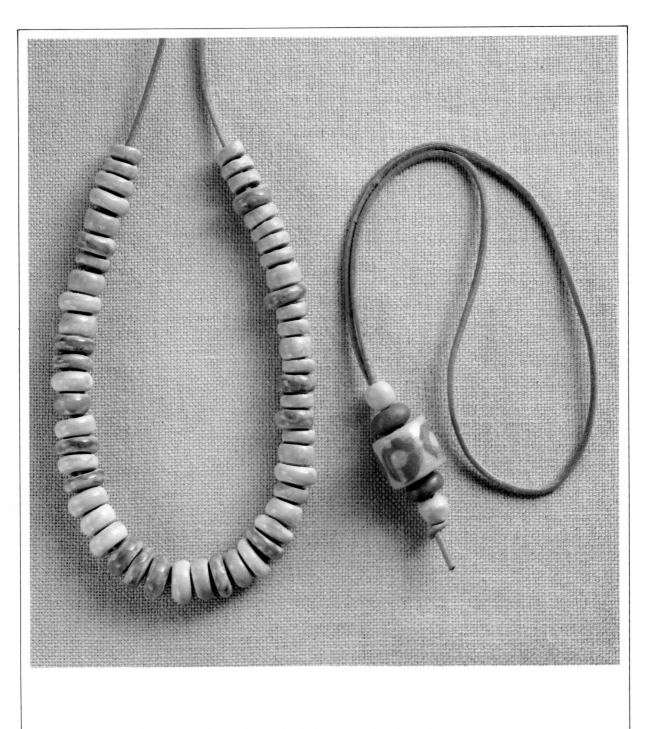

Necklace and pendant. *Squash small clay balls between thumb and index finger. Be careful to press evenly so that the edges do not crack. A smooth plastic clay without additives is best for clay jewellery. Colour while still damp with engobe or slip; fire and then glaze. The pendant in the illustration is made from remnants and leftovers. Threaded on a thong it makes a simple but effective personal ornament.*

Necklaces. To make the pieces in the lower necklace take a board and place two battens on either side as shown. Roll out a lump of clay between the battens until the rolling pin rests on them. Cut pieces of clay from the slab and roll the ends over a skewer. Seal the folded edge to the body with slip, make impressions in clay and colour with engobe. Allow the pieces to dry thoroughly before firing and glazing. The upper necklace was formed with pear-shaped pieces of clay cut from the slab. Both necklaces are interspaced with buttons squeezed from balls of clay.

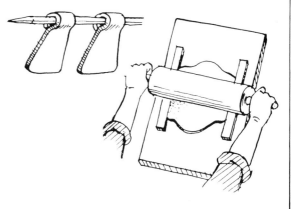

Thonged pendants. *These are fun and quite simple to make. Choose a shape for your pendant, then stamp it with different 'tools' – nails, pencils, or coins. Or you can make simple reliefs by fixing thin cut-out pieces of clay to your plaque with slip. Some variations are shown here.*

The pendant (bottom left) has been made with air-drying clay, coloured, then varnished. The lugs through which the thong is threaded have been left uncoloured and unvarnished.

Plant motifs

Making brooches, pendants or even miniature plaques decorated with plant motifs is simple and effective.

Search around for suitable plant material – leaves, ferns and plant skeletons are ideal. When you have decided what to use, put the plant material on a tabletop or slab, roll up a ball of clay and put it over the material. Press down on the clay with a slab of wood as illustrated, until the clay ball is squashed out to the thickness you want. If the clay cracks at the edges they can be smoothed down. Paint the flattened surface with coloured engobe so that the indentations the plant material has left are filled in. With water and a piece of soft cloth, sponge or cotton wool, wipe the surplus engobe from the face of the plaque.

The pieces below were decorated with engobe, fired, glazed, and fired again. Notice how the colouring has spread to the face of each plaque. The pieces on the next page were fired but left unglazed.

Brooches

Following the same principles for making the pendants opposite, you can make attractive brooches. These can be as large as you like, but remember large heavy brooches cannot be pinned to delicate fabrics – they are best seen on woollens. When designing, therefore, consider the material or dress on which they are to be worn. Brooches can be flat or slightly three-dimensional in form. A fixing pin has to be glued on to the back, so keep at least part of the back absolutely flat. Glue the pin on to the decorated brooch after firing or varnishing. The photograph on page 104 shows brooches decorated with leaf prints.

Brooches. These attractive brooches were decorated by pressing leaves into damp clay. The flattened surfaces were painted with coloured engobe so that the plant indentations were filled in and the brooches were then fired but left unglazed. A fixing pin was then glued to the back of the brooches.

Decorating clay

Decorated clay pot. *The versatility of clay gives a wonderful opportunity for imagination and individual expression. This pot has had the end of a key pressed into the rim to produce unusual and attractive markings. You could use it as a jar for kitchen utensils, or as a pen and pencil holder. This section illustrates different ways of decorating and marking clay.*

Before firing, a clay artifact can be decorated in a variety of ways. Decorating clay gives a wonderful opportunity for the imagination and individual expression. Models take on individuality: pots are raised from being mere artifacts to objects of craft and even art. The oldest form of decoration is made by marking the raw clay in one form or another. Listed below are some of the ways you can decorate your pieces by marking.

Fingers Pinching or impressing your fingers into the clay to produce deep impressions.

Objects Ruler edges, modelling tools, nails and screw heads, bits of machinery, keys, leaf forms, buttons, coins, twigs, shells – the list is almost endless. The slab of clay below has marks made in it by various objects. See if you can distinguish some of them.

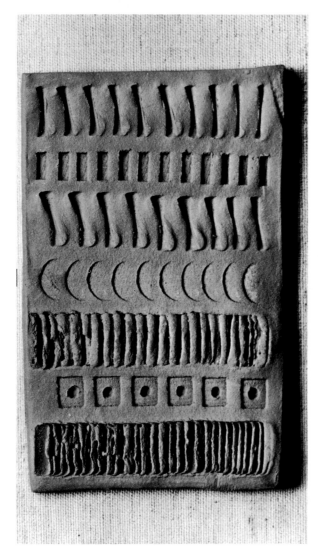

Stamps You can make your own stamps from a small piece of clay with the pattern in the end. Fire it and you have your stamp.
The two photos above show how stamps and reliefs can be pressed into plastic clay.

Beaters Butter pats and other flat and incised paddles can be used. Beat your pot carefully (support it from the inside with your free hand) to impart textures and patterns.

Rollers You can buy rollers which have a continuous pattern cut into the cylinder. Roll this on to the surface of your clay to obtain a pattern. Kitchen tools for making pastry will also offer continuous patterns.

Rolling When rolling out clay, put your lump of clay on sacking or a textured surface.

Sprigging This process consists of adding clay pieces to your formed pot. Shape and make a device or pattern in relief, then add it to your pot with slip. Experiment with different coloured clays.

Embossing The design was pressed firmly into the clay. It was then picked out with a contrasting oxide, and fired.

Incising Cut your clay with knives or modelling tools to create patterns and reliefs.

Inlay Cut away decorative areas and apply different coloured clays.

Piercing and cutting Pierce holes in a decorative pattern right through the wall of your pot, or cut away sections to produce a design. Or cut away thick parts of a round pot to give facets.

Sgraffito Scratch the surface of your clay with pointed tools, forks, or combs to produce an incised design. You can buy all sorts of tools to make different scratching marks on clay, but household implements are just as good!

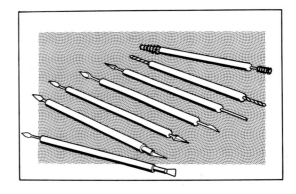

Oxides Different oxides can be rubbed or painted on to the surface of leather-hard clay to produce different tints.

Colouring the clay with different oxides The main oxides used for colouring can be bought at suppliers. They are iron, manganese, copper, cobalt, nickel antimony, and rutile (vanadium). Mix them into slip and knead the coloured slip into your lump of clay when preparing the clay. Suppliers' catalogues give useful information on the quantities you should use.

Engobe This is a slip made from a creamy clay mixture coloured with oxide. It is used for painting on to the surface of the unfired clay. Engobes can be bought from suppliers but are made quite easily from white clay and oxides. Stains, that are mixed from oxides, give a much wider range of colours, and are available in powder or tube form from pottery suppliers. These stains can be used like oxides. (Always read the manufacturers' instructions.)

If you want to make your own engobe, make a slip of white clay by mixing 3 oz (100 g) of white clay and adding water to it until it has a creamy consistency. Then add oxide in the proportions listed below:

4% red iron oxide	brown
1% cobalt oxide	medium blue
2% iron chromate	medium grey
3% copper oxide	medium green
10% vanadium stain	yellow
6% manganese dioxide	purple brown

Paint the engobe on with a brush when the clay is not quite leather-hard, or dip the whole pot into a bucket of coloured slip to colour the whole pot.

When the slip has dried, you can scratch out designs through the slip, leaving the unfired pot bare in places.

Decorated pots. *A selection of pots that have been decorated by using the various methods described in the previous pages. Some are embossed, others are incised. Some have been made with different coloured clays. Some have had designs painted on them with coloured slips, others have been dipped in slip. With the exception of the unsmoothed coil pot (centre left) all have been glazed.*

Glossary

Biscuit Pottery that has been fired to a condition where it is hard enough to glaze. Earthenware (qv) is porous, stoneware (qv) is impervious.

Body The word which all potters use for the clay they use to make their work.

Coiled pottery Hand-built pottery formed with rolls of clay which build up the form of the pot.

Combined water Chemically combined water in the molecular state with the clay molecules which is driven off when clay is fired to biscuit.

Dipping Glazing pottery by immersion in a container of glaze.

Earthenware Pottery made from clay which remains porous or unvitrified in the firing, which can be of as low a temperature as 800°C.

Engobe Another word for slip (qv), usually coloured, for applying to a pot as decoration.

Fettling To clean up the state of a raw clay pot.

Flux An ingredient used to lower the melting point of a glaze.

Frit An already fused mixture of flux and silica which is insoluble in water, (so as to render it non-poisonous).

Glaze A liquid suspension of a finely ground mixture of chemicals applied to biscuit ware to provide a glassy, impervious surface or coloured decorative effect when glaze or glost fired.

Glaze fired A firing process where the glaze materials applied to a pot will fuse to form a glasslike coating.

Glost Glaze or glazed. A glost firing is where glazed ware is completed.

Greenware Finished clay work that is not yet dry.

Grog Ground-down fired clay which is added to raw plastic clay to add texture or decrease shrinkage. Sand can also be used as a grog.

Kiln A high temperature oven made of refractory clay materials and used to fire clay.

Kiln furniture Shelves and props used for supporting objects in the kiln.

Orten cone A pyroscopic device made of ceramic that bends when heated to a precise temperature.

Plastic Clay capable of being worked into a shape which it will retain.

Raw Raw clay is unfired clay.

Refractory The property of resisting high temperatures.

Relief decoration Raised modelling on a pot (see sprigging).

Sgraffito A scratching technique used on unfired clay objects.

Short clay Clay that is not very plastic.

Shrinkage Contraction of the clay body as it dries out and/or during firing.

Slab pottery Hand-built pottery made by assembling rolled slabs of clay.

Slip Liquid clay mixture used for decoration and joining (see engobe).

Slurry A mixture of clay and water (see slip and engobe).

Sprigging Raised additions to the surface of raw pots.

Stoneware Pottery that is vitreous, non-porous and very hard, usually fired to above 1,200°C.

Under-glaze Decoration applied to a pot before glazing.

Vitrification Clay body that is fused through firing to become impervious.

Wedging Process of cutting and reforming a lump of clay preparatory to kneading, to give it a uniform texture.

Index